ANCHOR BOOKS

ANIMAL, VEGETABLE OR MINERAL

Edited by

David Foskett

First published in Great Britain in 1996 by
ANCHOR BOOKS
1-2 Wainman Road, Woodston,
Peterborough, PE2 7BU

HB ISBN 1 85930 359 5
SB ISBN 1 85930 354 4

Foreword

Anchor Books is a small press, established in 1992, with the aim of promoting readable poetry to as wide an audience as possible.

We hope to establish an outlet for writers of poetry who may have struggled to see their work in print.

The poems presented here have been selected from many entries. Editing proved to be a difficult and daunting task and as the Editor, the final selection was mine.

Poetry is becoming more and more popular each year and is written by many different people from all walks of life, which makes this book an enjoyable read from beginning to end.

All the poems included in this collection cover a wide range of subjects, views and personal experiences which everyone can relate to and understand.

So, find a quiet corner and expect to blow your mind with these poems by new and up coming poets.

I trust this selection will delight and please the authors and all those who enjoy reading poetry.

David Foskett
Editor

CONTENTS

Jesus Is My Lord And King	Winifred R Pettitt	1
My Best Friends	Thomas McIlroy	2
Wishing	M Constant	2
Max	Barbara Eggl	3
Leaving Home	Megan Walden	3
The Brothers - My Sons	Irene Patricia Kelly	4
Dreaming	Georgina Wells	4
Hand In Hand	Kim Montia	5
Home In My Town	Stephen Parkinson	5
One Of Those Days	June Roseman	6
Just Biking	Helen McLellan	7
A Walk In The Park	Kim Lee Rands	8
Beyond All Boundaries	Ingrid Riley	8
Night Tarts	T E Griffiths	9
Disaster In The Kitchen	Gillian Morrisey	10
A Bald Cook	Gillian Lewis	11
Getting Old	N A E Haxell	11
For Want Of Attention	Paul Newall	12
Jack	Sylvia Hall	12
A Plea	Doris Holland	13
Vikings!	Sybil Sibthorpe	14
Deep Down Desire	Barbara Jean Harrison	15
Aborted	Kevin John Mulligan	15
A Journey	Judith Garrett	16
Now I've Seen Everything	Florence MacLeod	17
(Heart And) Mind Love	Rune Brokstad	18
The Greatest Adventure	Debbie McQuiston	19
Lapping It Up	Mollie D Earl	20
Nature's Miracle	Margaret Jowset	20
Molly	Rhoda Greaves	21
My Cats	Christina Lewis	22
Unsighted But United	Edward John Bake	22
Cat In A Spin	Michael Jawornyj	23
Living Our Lives	Christine Joan Rouse	24
Faded Memories	Joyce M Hefti-Whitney	25
The Circle Of Life	Lloyd Noyes	26
Stranded	John Burge	27

A Gift From Above	Duncan MacFarlane	28
The Ballbreaker From Bath	Christopher A J Evans	28
Foreign Lady Of The Dance Floor	Simon Boothby	29
The New Arrival	William Howarth	30
Piggy	Beryl Smyter	30
Timbered	Dennis F Tye	31
For A Friend Who Died	Sheila Durbin	32
Summer's Ageing	Julie Whitworth	32
The Price Of Oil	Audrey Forbes-Handley	33
The Promised Land	N Stoddart	34
Manhunt	Eleanor West	35
Fantasy World	Vanessa Salt	36
Another Lonely Night	Selena Pearce	37
I Once New A Liberal Lady	Gerald Aldred Judge	38
Spring And The Panorama	J L Balchim	38
Some You Win	Teresa Kowal	39
New Vision Of Love	D Evans	39
The Borrowed Cat	Jean Thornton	40
Colours	Titarnia Payton Lubbuck	41
Uprooted	Adele E McCafferty	41
Mother's Love	Tracy Bell-Young	42
Song Of The Fairies	Edward Holmes	42
Growing-Up	Christine Thain	43
Who Knows	Rebecca Jones	44
Autumn	Jon Welch	44
Girl In The Picture	Michael Gardner	45
The World At My Feet	Gwyneth John	46
Mother's Love	Yvonne Stevens	46
Naughty Aunt Maude	Irene Ison	47
Humbugs And Peppermint Pipe	Sally Crook-Ford	48
Northern Winter	Ann Stewart	48
Where's Gem's Jersey	Jean Skates	49
Untitled	Carly Evans	50
Spiritual Healing	Eric Motson	50
Nature's Way	Margaret Laws	51
If Only	Joan Knapman	51

Shadows From The Heart	Mark Peter Evans	52
T	James Parry	53
Black Stuff	C R Wilkinson	53
A Friend From London	Martin Norman	54
Elliot	Barbara Ling	54
Time To Wake Up	Roger Brooks	55
My Computer Man	Jill Bramhall	56
Reflections	Ruby Ingham	57
Just Another Innocent	Christine Hulme	57
Mother Gazelle	Rose Bell	58
My Ever Expanding Waistline	Deborah Durbin	58
Children	June Mackillop	59
Who Took The Rain (Summer 95)	Irene Witté	60
Scenes Of Splendour	Helen J Lewis	61
My Heart Will Feel	I P Smyth	62
Bereavement	Lily Duncan	62
Insomnia	Drew Michaels	63
A Glimpse Of An Evacuee's Life	Hajar Javaheri	64
My Garden	Freda Nobes	65
Bring Back The Cat	F Oldfield	66
My Impulsive Husband	Jackie White	66
Will They Never Heed	R Nield	67
Looking For Love	Ann Harford	68
Spring	Camilla Clemens	68
When Shadows Fall	Malcolm Wilson Bucknall	69
Life Is Too Short	Rita Andain	70
Spring	O Stringer	70
My Heart And Soul Has Been Torn Away	Aliya Hanif	71
Street Beggar	Jenny Whitehead	72
Never Give Up	Alice Polley	73
As I Sleep, I Dream	Michael Spittles	73
Ode To Ole Ginger	Mary Kelly	74
Paradise	David Blair	75
Single Men	O O'Reilly	75

In Our Eye	Irene Hannaford	76
Health Or Wealth	A Usher	76
Loved Ones Lost	O M Godfrey	77
Conflict	Chris Throup	78
Still Life	S Keyes	79
What Then?	Rose Salter	80
Trees	Ann Fletcher Campbell	80
Surprise, Surprise	Louise Tilby	81
Totally Devoted To You	Janette Homer	82
A Fantasy	Betty Moir	82
Our Kids	Kathy Staggs	83
A Hero's Resting Place	Liam Quigley	84
Daisy	P Dyson	84
Don't Worry, Be Happy	Paul Wilkins	85
Lucky Win For Christmas	Professor Knutworthy	86
Silent Anger	S Amphlett	86
Don't Trust To Luck	Yona Geddes	87
Nobody Listens To		
The Old I'm Told	Susan Gerry	88
Good Times	R Beresford	89
The Tenth Life	Rosa Barbary	89
Spring Is In The Air	Jean McGovern	90
Sorrow In The Heart	Tracey Wheeler	91
My Regional Anthology	Stephen Butler	92
Life	Caroline Bunyard	92
Weather Of Time	Hilary Ann Torrens	93
Dreaming	Linsey Brown	93
RDA Gymkhana 1995	Violet M Corlett	94
Jack Frost	A Sebastian	95
Mad Cows' Disease	Joyce McArdle	96
Golden Hill (Alton)	G M Thorn	96
England, Oh My England!	Stephen P Jennings	97
Eternal Sleep	Lucille Hope	98
Being There	Ann F Rudy	99
Poles Apart	Pat Mear	100
Be Ye Ben Hur	Anita M Slattery	100
Space Child	Rodger Moir	101
My Friend Boris	Thomas Hartley	102

How Great Thou Art	Christina R Maggs	103
The Nun Who Had None	Donna Semark	104
The Mean Machine	Linda Miller	105
The Dream	Katherine Whiston	105
Racial Hatred	Christine Ward	106
Gazza Must Go	Alan Beasley	107
The Royal 'Boob'	Olivia Lambeth	108
To The Future	Beverley Waddington	108
I	David McShane	109
Public 'Fleeced'		
By Ostrich Farm	José Morgan	110
Mirror Image	Alex Southgate	110
Altered Perceptions	Ronald Guest	111
The Candle Flame	Paul Sanders	111
When I'm Gone	Sallie Sarjant Tugwell	112
Day Dreaming	Colin A Clouston	112
Did You Know?	Val Lacey	113
Mr Champ	Anna Beland	113
Limericks	Jack Howie	114
Summer	David Henry Bourne	115
The Cottage	Eileen Peggs	115
Portglasgow Toon	R Glass	116
The Step Back	Andy Mcpheat	117
The Rainbow	Christine McNaught	118
Epitaph For Old Nick	Margaret Nixon	119
My Oasis	David Brownley	120
Friends Will Be Friends	Monica R Rehill	121
To A Dear Friend	Margaret White	122
A Fragmented Life	Clive Bell	122
The Weather	Kathleen Jones	123
The Daybreak That		
Greets Tomorrow	Pat Judson	124
A Mysterious Guest	Marina Elizabeth Siddell	124
Dreaming	Leslie Daniels	125
Love Is	G W Bailey	126
In Memory Of Carl	Carl Bridgman	126
No Pity	Evelyn Farr	127
Untitled	J Nicholls	127

Denial	June Morland	128
A Close Friend	Rowland-Patrick Scannell	128
Who Has Comfort?	Anita Hanson	129
Friends	Margaret Andrews	130
Gold	John Young	131
Need	J A Lawrence	132
The Bird Not Seen	P S Joll	132
Myopia	Sandra A Merlini	133
First Love	J Hawkins	134
To Love A Friend	Francis Hinds	135
Always Remember - I Love You	D Fishwick	136
That Was Ricki Sylva	Malcolm Ross	137
My Friend Shirley	M I Johnstone	138
Food For Thought	Meg Pybus	138
With A Little Help	Meinir	139
Epitaph For Poets	Magdelena Hill (Deceased)	139
Man's Best Friend, The End?	Jeremy C W Bloomfield	140
'Clear View' Captain	David Powley	140
Drink	Matthew Ould	141
My Poem	Sheelagh Evans	142
God Bless The Bride And Groom	Gloria Wilkes	143
Set The Record Straight (The Beat Goes On)	Sandra Witt	144
Indecisive Moments	Victor Travis	145
Be Happy	Yvonne Powell	145
In Darkness Reign . . .	J Charles	146
Fox Tails	Bell Ferris	146
Monet	D T F Clifton	147
Oh How I Wish	Wendy Eaton	148
Curly's Cruel Bite	R J Collins	149
Lust - It Comes To Us All	D T Wicking	150
Oh Men Of Steel	Carole Lofthouse	150
Reiki	Marie Harte	151
Robert's Pride	Iris Ryder	152
My Wonderful PC	Sue Millward	152
Fairground	Stacey Priestley	153

Bombardment - Hartlepool	Alan Noble	154
Too Late My Love	Doreen Reynolds	154
Ouch!	G Carter	155
The Mountains Of Sierra Blanca	R Kumar	156
More Precious Than Gold	John Christopher Cole	157
My Thoughts For David	Rosemary Remy	158
The Journey Of Life	Frank Probett	158
My Mum	Doreen Day	159
Dreams	Eric Hope	160
Brewster	Theresa Corder	160
Leghorn Rackety	Colin N Howard	161
God Be With Me	Barbara Holme	162
Our Tourist Haven	Charles Ivor Morris	163
Discovery	Fred Tighe	164
Those Days Of Youth And Mischief	Fay Stanton	165
Times I Have Wandered	Andrew Quinn	166
Summer Breeze	G Crumpton	166
Reflections At 80!	Norman Wragg	167
Morning	Jean Parry	168
Turned Around	Jan Clarke	168
Listen	Catherine Venables	169
Lab Fever	F R Paulsen	169
Suicide	Alex D Sillifant	170
The Drummer Boy	George R Green	170
A Letter To Claire	Joanne Manning	171
The Never Ending Circle Of Life	Rita Hough	172
A Tale Of Natural Curls	Ann White	172
Abduction	Jazmin Jones	173
Memories Of Yester Years	Ella Fraser	174
Newton Charms	Paul Deavin	174
The Golden Years	R Scott	175
We Do Not Know	James H Cory	176
On The Scrap Heap	Alastair McGuinness	176
Poetry	Judy Thomas	177
Untitled	Lilian McCarthy	178

Holiday Madness	Jeannette Facchini	178
The Operation	Christopher Smithson	179
The Survivor	Daniela M Davey	180
Question And Answer	Beryl Stockman	180
Our Island	Ivy Barnes	181
Neo-Geordie Blues	M E Ord	182
My Silent World!	Laura Weston	183
Blandford Railway Track	Janet Poulsen	184
Sparkles	P Jones	184
Down The Tube	Jean Beith	185
Dirty Totton Town	Patrick Art Cooper-Duffy	186
Ken's Room	Ando	186
Abused Children	C Holmes	187
West Dorset Churchyard	Jennifer Ackerman	188
Come To My House - Please	Marvin Jones	189
Home	I Burnell	190
A Bride And Her Mother	Carol Shaikh	190
My Boys	Pam Fitzjohn	191
Landlubbers	Eileen Forrest	192
Ode To Margaret	R M Moulton	192
Who Is It?	Lara Allen	193
Bingo Barmy	Tommy Warburton	194
Starting Over	M Robinson	194
The Holiday	Barry L J Winters	195
Dream On	Charles Owusu	196
I Dream Every Day	Parveen Dharr	197
The Twilight Time	Dee Lean	198
In Defence Of The Fallen	George Kitchen	199
My Burmese Boy - Baggy	Samantha Kerr	200
Circles	M T Bridge	201
Man	E P Devereux	202
Lepers	John Farrell	202
The Waggon And Horses	Jacey	203
Hills	Cathy Hudson	203
For Life Is Like		
A Ticking Clock	June Downie	204
Revenge	J Harazny	205
Feeling Fine	Bruce Fisher	206

Your Eye's A Mirror	Deneaze Tyrrell	207
If Given One Wish	Julie Hunt	208
Happy?	Pauline Jones	208
Just One More Time	Sue Watts	209
Night Shadows	Denise Threlfall	210
The Simple Poet	Norman Neild	211
Loneliness	Ruth Calder	212
Insistent Words!	Pat Rees	213
Me?	Helen Pisarska	214
Brian's Nightmare	A M Pearson	215
The Blessed Sinner	Jagdeesh Sokhal	216
Expensive Dreams	Alison Haysman	217
Untitled	Rachel Todd	218
Aspiring Dream	Marion Pollitt	218
Loneliness And Regrets	J Dell	219
The Christmas Light	T MacNaughton	220
A Nation's Flagship	S A Wilson	221
The Prisoner	Patricia J Pratt	222
Bewildered Spirit	May Strike	223
Connaire	Geraldine Rollins	224
The Scenery Above	Tracy Hoar	224
Haven't Got A Minute	Phyllis Bromfield	225
At Last Peace Is Found	Katrina	226
What Do You See	M Evans	227
Drugs	Jane Taylor	228
My Problem	J Rogers	228
My Hobby	Sian Hartland	229
Round About	J Morgan	230
Old Nick	Jean Carter	231
Why	Paula Cronick	232
Advice To Newlyweds	Freddy McDonnell	233
Xmas In London	Miriam Eissa	234

JESUS IS MY LORD AND KING

Jesus is my Lord and King
Songs of praise to Him I'll sing.
Jesus is my helper, friend.
God, from Heaven, His Son did send,
Came to save the world from sin,
So that we all could enter in,
Safe, in God's dear Heaven, above,
Sharing in His wondrous love.

Jesus Christ is coming again.
Jesus is coming back to reign.
He will gather His children in,
Cleansed by His blood from all their sin.
Jesus Christ is the only door,
He can save you for evermore.
Come to the Saviour. Don't delay.
Time's running out. He could come today.

Oh, what a meeting that will be,
When our blessed Lord we'll see.
Many loved ones who've gone before,
They will be with us for evermore.
Going first, to our Lord they'll fly.
We'll follow on, with rapturous cry,
Guided home, by His own dear hand,
Borne to Glory, in His Heavenly land.

Winifred R Pettitt

MY BEST FRIENDS

My best friends
I like to play with them
we like to play rounders
they like to play
in my tent
so do I.

Their names are
Craig, Barrie and Stuart
They're my best of friends.

Thomas McIlroy (6)

WISHING

I wish that I could roam the world far and wide,
To find someone, like you by my side,
But I know that it would be in vain
As nothing will never now be the same,

Since the first day you made me your wife
You shared and taught me so much in this life
That my happiness came from the love you gave me,
And it showed for the whole world to see.

The love you gave me was so honest and true
Never will there be another you,
I know that you are free from pain
That I am selfish and wanting you with me again

If only you could have a few more years to spare
For us to have more happy years to share,
I love you and still want you here
As I miss you so very much my dear.

M Constant

MAX
Born 3.6.1993

You want to taste the whole world
with your tongue

the sun, the sky, the salty ocean
the sweetness of the night
the dusty streets of summer
the noise, the depression

You want to taste love's colour
it melts on your tongue
you take my hand and laugh

Barbara Eggl

LEAVING HOME

'Got 'im', gnash the chromium plated teeth
and I gnash mine as clutched in the metal jaws
he pulls away

Down the road and into life away from me
precious flesh and blood let loose.
An awful day

Free from needs that held him bound to us
he welcomes the beckoning world outside,
rejoices in the fray

Breaking the loving cobweb dense and soft
all-comers challenged face to face.
We wouldn't have him stay

He never saw my tears, my back was turned.
'Don't go, don't go,' I whisper through closed lips
and smile him away

Megan Walden

3

THE BROTHERS - MY SONS

Beautiful voices, in childhood unexplored.
In one, an actor's face,
If not by choice then by design,
Dark-eyed sensitivity,
Astronomy, musicality.
The others, fairer by sport obsessed.
Dark-eyed sensitivity,
Musicality, practicality.
'Three Musketeers,'
'One for all,
And all for one.'

Irene Patricia Kelly

DREAMING

As I sit and watch you sleeping in your bed
I wonder what thoughts are going through your head.
Are you dreaming of a wonderland.
The bright warm sun glimmering on the sand.
I see you smile at something in your wonderland
What can it be I long to know!
Should I wake you I don't think so
I'll leave you to dream
For in my mind's eye
I can see your wonderland
With its soft white clouds
And its glimmering sands
So sweet dreams my child
Until the morning light
Safe in your bed
            all cosy and warm.

Georgina Wells

HAND IN HAND

Northern Ireland's mothers are united by their tears
Their prayers for each son's safety and the depth of all their fears
The knot inside their stomachs during marches and parades
Dreading offspring from these confrontations be conveyed
To hospitals, to prison cells or yet to be interred
Within the swollen cemeteries where wailed laments are oft' times heard
Teaching every child that they must guard against their tongue
Take care to whom they speak in any neighbourhood they're flung
Northern Ireland's mothers walk hand in hand with grief
And each one prays to God for a time to sigh relief.

Kim Montia

HOME IN MY TOWN

Coming home, from holiday into my town at night.
Is so different to going away when it's light and bright.
Travelling from my town, to another, is exciting and new.
What I will miss is my friends and a cuppa brew.
Neighbours which ask you in for a cuppa, can be a pain
When what's on your mind is supper and time to relax the brain
In my home, I'm indoors.
Even behind closed doors, I'm here with a telly a full belly and
                                                resting my feet
So I shouldn't complain about nothing happening and no-one to meet.
What happens around here I do not know
If I opened the curtains I would see snow.
It could be a whiter, brighter, town if I cared what went on.
Then I would know about people calling with the latest con
I might take note if people called round for my support for a by-pass
Then people, tourists and passers by would miss my town going straight past
Onto a new road ahead, leading forward
Away from towns where people are bored.
I wonder are the grass verges greener on the other side.

Stephen Parkinson

ONE OF THOSE DAYS

Oh what a fuss, oh what a to do
The hoover's broken and it's almost new!
I must look for the guarantee
Now where have I put it, where can it be

I can't think where I put that slip
Oh my back is beginning to give me gip
A brush and shovel is not the same
To clean the dust in my wee hame

The clock on the wall is ticking away
They'll soon be here, oh why today!
I'd better put the kettle on
A spark, oh no there's something wrong

I'll lay the table and then I'll look
For a solution in my DIY book
I'm sure it will point to the culprit, the fuse
Or else this appliance is no damn use

Everything's ready, as neat as can be
Kettle is working, clever old me,
Table is set, now what can I do
Relax, calm down they'll arrive at two

I'll just pop to the loo and wash my face
I'm fine for time, everything's in place
At ten to two, the doorbell rings
This bathroom door is stuck, oh jings!

Take a deep breath, and pull the door
What's that I heard fall on the floor
There's a letter lying on the mat
It was only the postman, thank God for that

At five past two, my guests arrive
The new neighbours, Mary, Jane and Clive
Formalities over, relax, have our tea
It's been one of those days, don't you agree!

June Roseman

JUST BIKING

The slashing and burning is over, a tarmac'd
surface runs through,
the deepest and darkest, black jungle, just the
road, and the sky, now, there's you.

No sound apart from his breathing, no light, apart
from the stars,
No movement, apart from my heartbeat, the jungle
alone, is now ours.

Fear is fast in arising, the key to the bike's in
his hand
the tarmac road we've been riding, disappears
like water through sand.

I manage to gasp out my terror, the key goes
once more in the lock,
the engine purrs louder with pleasure while the lights on the bike seem to mock
. . .

My horror as we ride through the jungle, a
rainforest drive for a lark,
Along the Bruce Highway in Queensland
two pommies, plus bike, in the dark!

Helen McLellan

A WALK IN THE PARK

The bare wooden skeletons,
of what once used to be,
ripe, luscious vegetation.

Bottle fades to lime,
Burgundy blends into rust,
Copper melts to mustard,
And cherry mingles with alburn.

Hedgerow alters,
Fruit and berries dry up,
Offerings become scarce.
And the undergrowth swells,
with the colours of autumn.

Kim Lee Rands

BEYOND ALL BOUNDARIES

We live and breathe an atmosphere
Where mysterious and dark secrets rule,
Unknown to our conscious thoughts.
Elements are hidden, linked up,
A part of our mind and body
Which we cannot cage nor control.
The threads of our spirit are sensors
Which leave our bodies, give us visions,
Reaching out beyond all boundaries.
It is the pulse of our future.
In vain we search for the right key
To break open the door to Paradise,
Where treasures lie in our far-reaching thoughts,
A hidden link connecting Earth and Heaven.

Ingrid Riley

NIGHT TARTS

Recipe rhymes from Delia
all assemble at the kitchen parade.
Pinches of salt for cookhouse gambles
where Vertumnus eyes Pomona
over Alfred's cinders.
O' what a lovely caper,
four and twenty blackbirds sing into
a pie funnel and wives with knives
spoil for pastry honours.
Doughnut galley begins the battle,
divorced eggs waltzed around the
coagulating bowl, and rolling pins
tame the doughy chicanes.
Loaves and fishes not enough,
will kitchen prima donna blend her
culinary charms into another
Antoinette gaffe.
Choux to fit all tastes - Mrs Beaton!
Laced with notables I see,
I wonder if Madeira will be topless again.
Pestle rattles mortice in annoyance
and hot oven ardours rise irresistibly.
Now watch those shortbread tiddly winks
leap into their biscuit barrel,
pass the billy-can
dad's army can march on its stomach.
Crept down that night to the Manchester tarts,
their sweet enticement drew my last resistance,
phew!
Empty cases left to the morning sun.

T E Griffiths

DISASTER IN THE KITCHEN

I've got to cook a meal for four
What can I cook that's new
I know I'll do a chicken dish
And to start a bowl of soup

The starter very easy it came out of a tin
And I prepared a nice big salmon
To set in aspic jelly
But to my dismay it fell from the plate
And landed on its belly

I stuffed the chicken with my eyes closed
I couldn't bear to look
What was I doing
To this poor little chook

I made a dish of summer fruits
It really looked a treat
Until piping on the cream
The dish fell on my feet

I slipped upon some melon balls
And fell down on the floor
I got up hurt and angry
And made straight for the door

I went down to the fish shop
And got cod and chips for four.

Gillian Morrisey

A BALD COOK

Oh, why do men's hair disappear?
A hereditary constitution of fear
You comb your baldness day and night
Hoping it will grow back in sight
You try to cover up your crowns
By covering strands and grooming down
The roots are there beneath the skin
The hair will grow from the soul within
Why put up with all the rude words
Try stimulation; rice fruit and herbs
If you only know how cute you look
Baldness is in the trendy cook
Beneath baldness comes the brains
So unlock your biological root trains;
And there will be a crowning glory
That is hidden cooking in this story.

Gillian Lewis

GETTING OLD

You tell me I am getting old, I tell you that's not so!
The 'house' I live in is getting old, that of course, I know.
It's been in use a long, long time, it's weathered many a gale;
I'm really not surprised you think it's getting somewhat frail.
The colour changing on the roof, the windows getting dim;
The walls a bit transparent and looking rather thin;
My house is getting shaky, but my house isn't *me*.
My few years left, can't make me old, I feel I'm in my youth!
Eternity does lie ahead, a life of joy and truth!
You only see my house outside, which is all that most folk see;
You tell me I am getting old! You've mixed my 'house' with *me*.

N A E Haxell

11

FOR WANT OF ATTENTION

Today my mind went wandering
and sat down by a tree:
it begged the flowers humbly
'please come and sit with me,
These are the days of joy and splendour!
These are the times that care!
So come and rest awhile just here,
and fix me with your stare.'
But nature is because it is,
and won't be told what it should do.
'The sun still shines,' the flowers said,
'Why should we sit with you?'
My mind could find no answer,
no simple reason why;
so it sat, and cried when the sun went out
and watched those flowers die.

Today my mind went wandering
and sat down by a tree.
But the flowers wouldn't sit with it,
so it came back to me.

Paul Newall

JACK

Jack you are so special
We've known that from the start
A gift to Nik and Alison
But you had a poorly heart

The wonders of modern medicine
And the skill of the surgeon's hand
Has made you well and whole again
You're so precious my little man

I'm looking to the future
As over the years you grow
May God grant you his love and blessings
And on you his gifts bestow

It really won't be all that long
Until you are a young man
I'm glad you are my grandson
I'm so proud to be your nan

Sylvia Hall

A PLEA

Jesus wants me for a sunbeam
He's on a loser here
I'm no more like a sunbeam
Than a year old bottle of beer
My blood pressure's not as it should be
My joints creak like mad
The years that are past and forgotten
Are the best that I've ever had.

I can't dig a bed in the garden
I did plant a packet of seeds
I don't really know what happened
They all came up as weeds
If I go far I have to take taxis
I can't walk a lot any more
And when I get out of the taxi
I could hit my head on the door

So if I'm required as a sunbeam
Please agree to break all the rules
Just make me fifty years younger
And give me a win on the pools

Doris Holland

VIKINGS!

Across the wild sea, row hard, me lads
And wrestle the rolling tide;
Though arms are aching and muscles breaking
And the sea is vast and wide.
But we'll murder rape and pillage in every little village
And we'll strike 'em down in cottage and town.

The wind is howling and storming, lads,
And it's cold on the bleak North Sea;
The boat is bucking like a stallion wild
As the waves run high and free.
And we'll murder rape and pillage in every little village
And we'll strike 'em in cottage and town.

The rain is sleeting in a sullen stream
Coming down from a grey dark sky
And your muscles glisten with sweat and rain
As the oars go dipping dipping by.
So we'll murder rape and pillage in every little village
And we'll strike 'em down in cottage and town.

Now the shore's in sight, we've made it lads,
Get your swords in your hands readily
But before we step ashore, just one thing lads
Burn the boat on the rolling sea.
Then we'll murder rape and pillage in every little village
And we'll strike 'em down in cottage and town.

We have burned our boat on the cold grey sea
And there's no turning round and going home.
Here's where we'll live or here's where we'll die,
And we'll fight for a place to call our own.
Now we'll murder rape and pillage in every little village
And we'll strike 'em down in cottage and town.

Sybil Sibthorpe

DEEP DOWN DESIRE

I often imagined a trip to New York,
but aeroplanes scare me and cause me to balk.
Although hustle and bustle is not really my scene,
New York is a place I wished I had been.
To tour Greenwich Village for art and design
and mix with people of similar mind.
The financial position is decidedly grim
and unfavourable health, the chances are thin.
Despite the desire the country appeals
to resign myself to what destiny deals.
A quieter abode appeals to the senses,
woods, green pastures and rustic fences.
So Scotland it is for future dreams,
providing of course I have the means.
Adventurous once, but not any more,
just a country person, a bit of a bore.

Barbara Jean Harrison

ABORTED

Although in truth I'm not yet born, they've
already decided my fate;
They've examined my mum and done the tests
and know I've got a heart rate.
Because I'm not yet visible it's assumed I'm
unaware what's going on;
But they're sadly wrong, cos I've heard them say
'We don't want a son.'
So as the bin is wheeled in, the operation
is carried out;
If only I could see the look on their face as
they realise, 'I don't have a spout!'

Kevin John Mulligan

A JOURNEY

They told me all I needed was a fine summer
How could they possibly foretell
that strange and sad things happen in the summertime as well.
The fevered heat of summer cuts as deep as any shower of winter's
                                                          discontented sleet.
But still they told me all would be well
in the long fine summer they had foretold.
And the days were long and fine and as beautiful as gold.

So I set out upon a journey
a journey into the deep recesses of the mind
a journey I wanted to be limitless and beyond time.
And every day I laboured like an over anxious tourist
caught in the grip of a fabulous trip
on a cut price ticket to the Holy Land.
Imagining the climb to the highest peak of illumination
where I thought to find a sign
a glimpse of the eternity.
A breath from this mystery did pass through me
from the tremulous breeze through the leaves on the trees in this
                                                          fine summertime.

But the feeling was caught
trapped by the shadow of the thought
that came between me and the discovery that might have been.
But still I relentlessly pursued this longed for reality I had been told about
where me is not in the verb 'to be'
only a beautiful sense of unity
Thy Kingdom come, Thy Kingdom is.
But the summer that was fine and long passed away in the ephemeral
                                                          breeze and was gone
leaving me without the prize gift.

For it has been written down as many times as there are thorns in the crown
the way of the everlasting song is an arduous one and long
and I had only just begun.

Judith Garrett

16

NOW I'VE SEEN EVERYTHING

Just after 3am on the ninth of November, nineteen eighty seven,
I woke with a start from a noise as if coming from Heaven,
It sounded like an iron chain dragging across the roof,
To put it mild I was frightened, it was very spoof,
I waited to see what sound would come next,
Nothing, I jumped out of bed very vexed,
I gazed in the darkness out into the night,
Then I was transfixed by this colossal light,
This brilliant flashing light hung in the air,
I knew at once it was a UFO, uncanny glare,
Nothing on earth could have stayed on one spot,
When I tell people all they say is 'I'm talking rot'
Nobody wants to believe it, too scared or what?
It's exciting to see this thing so terrific,
And so very galling that no one will believe it,
At first I thought they were all daft,
Until I suddenly began to laugh,
These flashes could be sending pictures back into space,
And what will they see? A nose on a window and my face,
My hair all tangled, no teeth, with eyes all amazed,
They have travelled millions of miles to see me dazed,
They came all this way to film this earth,
And I've made a horror film for what it's worth,
If ever they return from goodness knows where
The first thing I'll do is to comb my hair.

Florence MacLeod

(HEART AND) MIND LOVE

. . . Then I closed my eyes
Came out of my daily disguise
My thoughts disappeared into empty air
The subconscious created situations so bare

I saw a lot of beautiful things
Beautiful as any love song John Lennon sings
Sweat pouring as the sun was shining
Right atmosphere for some reclining

Suddenly a mysterious shadow appears
Fortunately not the beast everyone fears
But an incredible beauty
And she called me a cutie

After hours of relaxing, flirting and talking
The two of us stand up and start walking
To her hotel suite
To find our feet

No doubt, we were in love and so we knew
Therefore it was perfectly clear what we should do
Always be together
Regardless the weather

I said: 'I really love your body and your mind,
I'm sure you're the loveliest woman, I'll ever find.'
'By the way, my name is Rune B.'
In a Danish accent she said: 'I'm Helena C.'

Rune Brokstad

THE GREATEST ADVENTURE

I am on the Greatest Adventure,
That there can ever be,
It started when my Lord,
Held out His hand to me.

It started with the Bible,
A wondrous and living book,
He opened up the pages,
And said, 'Come, take a look.'

The words inside made no sense,
I couldn't understand,
What did He have to do with me,
This Man from a foreign land?

But I accepted His challenge,
He said, He would love me true,
He said, 'I will take you on adventures,
In everything you do.'

It's been six years now,
That I have been with Him,
It's been a great adventure,
Learning what causes me to sin.

It hasn't always been easy,
We've had a laugh and shed a tear,
But it's the greatest adventure,
Learning how to live without fear.

So now I'm asking all of you,
Join this adventure with me,
It starts when my gentle Lord,
Holds out His hand to thee.

Debbie McQuiston

LAPPING IT UP

I'd love to go to Lapland
To see the tundra and the snow
Where reindeer race across the land
Against nightime's eerie glow.

I'd love to see the Laplanders
As they fish beneath the ice
With line and hook and harpoon
Which all their need suffice.

I'd love to see the Husky teams
Pulling sledges o'er the snow,
And Polar bears a'playing
Along an iceberg flow.

I'd love to see the Northern lights
Like searchlights passing by
With rainbow curtains swaying
Across the great wide sky.

I'd love to go to Lapland
And see the midnight sun
Where day is just a twilight
And night is never done.

Mollie D Earl

NATURE'S MIRACLE

As a child my father would recite poetry to me
I feel appreciation when I see the daffodils wild and free

Our future is mapped out for us, we grow from that seed
Creation transforming we bloom, and we fulfil a need

My family's been important to me, but now I can come first
Now I've achieved writing poetry, wine in glass Tim I've a thirst.

You can express through verse and rhyme exactly how you feel
Create, expand another's need, with wisdom and appeal.

I can show my gratitude for my published work out this year
I've moved on as there was someone out there ready to hear.

Margaret Jowset

MOLLY

It was there.
Red and purple, and mine.
Just lying
'What is it?'
I spoke - but not really.
Encapsulated in a moment,
bonding.
So fragile,
So precious.
I touched it.
I touched her.
My creation. The gift to nullify all others.
Overcome by a love unknown,
Tiredness vanishes.
I would not sleep - just look.
With an indescribable pride not even Olympic gold could match.
I did not cry. It was not that kind of meeting.
United in blood and nakedness.
That cherished introduction.
You have forgotten in seconds -
What I will take to the grave.

Rhoda Greaves

MY CATS

Cats cats cats
Everywhere you go
In the kitchen
Upstairs
Downstairs
No no no!

Cats outside
Lazy cats in the room
Sitting on the sofa,
Chairs as well . . .
Bang goes the plates
On the kitchen floor,
Smash!

It makes me scream!
I had a dream
All the cats had stolen the cream.

Christina Lewis (8)

UNSIGHTED BUT UNITED

Fog comes silently thro' the night
No sun or stars are in sight
No wind or breeze to fly a kite
All is hazy, there is no light
We walk unsteady on the ground
We listen for each earthly sound
The traffic is slow
        Drivers cannot see
The funny shapes
        Of you and me
So go away you nasty fog
I'll always rely on my trusty dog

Edward John Bake

22

CAT IN A SPIN

I enjoy living with my owner - the lovely Miss Dee,
But last week something terrible happened to me.

And I ended up in a sorry state,
With my lives reduced to eight.

I'd just arrived home as usual via the flap,
Having been out all night - I was looking forward to a nap.

I gently sneaked into the small kitchen,
The washing machine door was open, so I climbed in.

I thought the soft clothes in this warm place would make
an ideal bed,
It turned out to be my biggest mistake instead.

I was almost asleep when Miss Dee locked me in and switched on,
And before I could miaow she had gone.

I started to spin round and round - with her black skirt
And sweater,
And all the time getting wetter and wetter.

I must have passed out after that,
I just remember the vet telling Miss Dee that I'm a
Lucky cat.

I've now got a soft and shiny coat,
But still have a bit of a sore throat.

The kitchen is now out of bounds,
And I smell sweetly of washing powder - as I go about
My rounds.

Michael Jawornyj

LIVING OUR LIVES

We are born into this world,
Not knowing what we shall be told,
A life of breathing and thinking too,
For us all to start anew.

Everyday a new leaf unfolds,
For us to learn if we may be so bold,
Experiencing things in a different way
Through every hour of each new day.

We learn to talk we learn to read,
Hopefully not to learn the greed,
We learn to laugh and sing and play,
Through the specialness of each day.

We are taught to exercise and dance and enjoy,
What comes natural to girls and boys,
We experience lots of life's pleasure,
Including a way of enjoying our leisure.

We learn to say our Prayers to the Lord Jesus,
Who we know is there, the Presence of His Love and Healing
Makes us know these special feelings.

We learn to work apart from play,
Showing how we adapt in a wonderful way,
Our life goes on to build us families and hope,
That we always learn the right way to cope.

Christine Joan Rouse

FADED MEMORIES

The residential home for retired gentlefolk sat like a sandstone Taj Mahal
Covered in ivy hiding the grime and the smoke.
Its assorted residents were passed their prime, beyond any sell by date.
For the most they sat with a vacant far away look in their tired eyes,
What were their thoughts? Were they of hope? Love? Or hate?
Mabel was special.
She had lived her life to the full. Memories of her youth, of tea dances,
The Charlston, that heart throb Valentino, her life was never dull.
She still dyed her hair bright red! Her wrinkled lips a blur of red, refusing
Adamantly to wear slippers (against the rules) even though her knees killed
Her, she trotted around in high heels instead!
She sat in a middle of a row of high backed chairs, smiling and chatting
About the good times, greeted in return by solemn and vacant stares.
She loved Xmas. Adored Easter and couldn't wait for new year!
The years had gone so quickly she'd no idea how long she'd been here?
Family? None to speak of. 'I'm too stroppy to die!' she'd sigh.
But alone in the quiet of her little room she'd sit and remember and cry.
She'd cry for Bill, or was it Jim? Whoever he was she'd fond memories of
Him. How he'd sent her long love letters from somewhere out in France,
How he'd vowed they'd wed, 'first possible chance.'
But he never returned. Like so many others. Dads, uncles, lovers and
                                                    brothers
Now as she looked at his faded photo all rag eared and torn,
Recollecting her love for him and felt uplifted and warm.
Tomorrow it's her birthday! 100! She'll get a telegram from the Queen!
There'll be joyous celebrations for Mabel, this lovely, generous, warm
And loving forgotten . . . has been.

Joyce M Hefti-Whitney

THE CIRCLE OF LIFE

Inquisitively kicking, anguishing before birth
Aimless so I thought.
The glory and the splendour, God's thoughts I adorned,
Even now, by His blood I've been bought.

White light, voices ecstatic,
The angels have embraced me with their wings
My mother draws me to her breast
Assuring, soothing words of comfort.

Jungle warfare, spiritual warfare, the ultimate challenge
Though it sets your heart aflame.
The Lord God on high will deliver me,
He says He knows my name.

Degrees, diplomas, competitive factions to quell,
The Midas touch, the killing touch,
The touch of wisdom upon the worlds
Commitment to the Holy one offers escape from hell.

Old age, grey hair, debt free,
Sounds of grandchildren echoing family histories,
The circle of life repeating the circle of life,
Expectancy of eternal life comforts me.

The one who sits on the circle of the earth
Has been through it all before.
We both obtained the glory;
That my friends, is not folklore.

Lloyd Noyes

STRANDED

Stranded in the desert, was just my luck,
Towed off the track, with a broken down truck.

No one knows, how long I will have to stay,
With just my truck, to give me some shade.

Plenty of water to drink and food to eat,
Though bully and biscuits, is not a feast.

Shading my eyes with both hands,
Wherever I look, there is nothing but sand.

In the dark while trying to sleep,
Silly thoughts, in my mind start to creep.

Would someone sneak up, during the night,
Try to kill me with a dagger or knife.

Trying hard to keep alert and wide awake,
I slept next morning till it was very late.

Getting my brew can out, to make a mug of tea,
My flesh started to tingle, someone was behind me.

Grabbing my rifle, just in case, I turned and saw the face,
Of an Arab, who turned out to be, not a menace

In his outstretched hand he was holding an egg,
He wanted to swap it for some bully and biscuits instead.

Where did he come from, where did he go?
To tell you the truth, I never did get to know.

Often the thought enters my head,
Where in the hell did he get that egg?

That is the end of that little episode,
As back to the war I was gladly towed.

John Burge

A GIFT FROM ABOVE

A gift from above, there came a baby full of love,
Douglas is little Douglas is fine,
Douglas is a boy divine, sent from Heaven when we
Were down, shining like a beam upon a crown
See him (among a crowd) happy and cheerful.
He is sincere and playful, Douglas is little
Douglas is fine Douglas is a boy divine.
God blessed us with love for a child,
That stretches from the Clyde to the Nile
There is wondrous sights in every mile
But only Douglas has that perfect smile
We tried to save our treasure for Heaven
But this gift, a jewel of a child, has made
Our life worth living, so high above
On your mighty throne Lord we can
Only thank you with our love.

Duncan MacFarlane

THE BALLBREAKER FROM BATH

There's a female wrestler called Kath,
Who's nicknamed the 'Ballbreaker from Bath.'
One day she took on a man,
Who labelled himself, 'Battling Stan.'
It was Stan who started the brighter,
Despite being shorter, and lighter,
But Kath reached out strongly and gripped.
As poor Stan, went wet-eyed, and tight lipped,
He now knows, how she came by her name,
Departing the ring, squeaky-voiced, on a cane.

Christopher A J Evans

FOREIGN LADY OF THE DANCE FLOOR

The truth of my life laid in that night,
When I kissed a foreign lady on the dance floor
Twas a kiss of beauty, love or more,
A kiss I shall remember for evermore.

And they say true love is greater than friendship
Well they must surely be of the night
When hours I spent to communicate in dark light
As I watched your eyes which never left my sight.

Oh foreign lady of the dance floor
That music plays my mind
Out of all times with other
You were my greatest find.

I know of all the songs and poems of love
And to say that at least we are part of this
Is to take away our human rights
As you were the only one I saw in my sight

And foreign lady of the dance floor
There were feelings expressed so true
Each kiss I gave was sacred
And yours must have been from the heavens so true.

As you see lady I was the lonesome shepherd
Until you revealed my name
And I had the image of a rag and bone man
Until you declared my shame.

You were the foreign lady dressed in English clothes
Which was your Danish accent cover
And your smile was goodbye
But if there were any, it was you my *lover*.

Simon Boothby

THE NEW ARRIVAL

When a child is born into this world
It does not matter if boy or girl
For there are people standing around
With a mask on and a white gown.

The father and friends are waiting near
With their hearts held in fear
Is it a boy or is it a girl
As they wait with their head in a whirl.

Maybe it will be a pigeon pair
Then they will have a son and heir
One to be a dutiful son
The other one to be a beautiful mum.

All these people waiting there
Some of them will say a silent prayer
For they are waiting to hear that first cry
It will sound like a sweet lullaby.

All at once they heard a cry
And those waiting there gave a sigh
For now arrives that bundle of joy
Is it a girl or is it a boy?

William Howarth

PIGGY

A piggy went
  A snorting
On a bright and
  Breezy day.

He snorted at
  The sheep in the field
But they just
  Turned away.

He snorted at
  The cows a milking
But they just
  Blinked an eye.

So Piggy got
  Fed up with this
And rolled in
  Mud with sigh!

Beryl Smyter

TIMBERED

A forthright young chap named Kent,
Found he was astronomy-bent.
Read every book that he could get
But gained no satisfaction yet!
So putting the books upon a shelf,
He said: 'Must go to space, myself!'

To his workshop he did go,
Thus now begins a tale of woe.
Constructed he a spaceship fine
Well conceived of strongest pine.
Daily worked hard as he could
Building there his craft of . . . wood!

Came the moment awaited - long,
The young chap he burst into song.
His task complete, he wheeled it out
With joyous outburst he did shout.
'Farewell all! . . . I'm off to Mars!'
But ship blew up! Saw naught but *Stars!*

Dennis F Tye

FOR A FRIEND WHO DIED

He is gone beyond the curtain
That hangs at the edge of the world -
We may reach that edge unwitting
It may even be here and now -
Many years he was with us
Sailing through dark days and bright days.
He felt the heave and plunge
Of mid-Atlantic surges
And tasted salt spray on the wind;
Heard the harsh cries of sea-birds.
He saw the islands of spice,
He glimpsed the glittering iceberg
And the wing-span of the Albatross,
The aurora's mystic dance;
But now - intrepid voyager -
He has gone beyond the curtain
Into the heart of light.

Sheila Durbin

SUMMER'S AGEING

The semi-circular shades of a tree,
A lawn thick with daisies and buttercups.
Looks across overgrown pathways
To small bungalow buildings.
Two seats left out from long ago,
Stare empty into woodland.
Where rich and varied bird song
Fills the air.
The heat of the sun warms the grass.
'Til we reach the cool of the shade at last.

Julie Whitworth

THE PRICE OF OIL

The last few miles of hopeful flight towards my welcome nesting place . . .
My wings reflect the morning light, and all the others of my race
Are gathering now. Another spring beckons us home to preen and feed,
To choose a place to lay our eggs where every year we come to breed,
To raise our chicks, to carry on our part in Nature's sacred chain
Of life . . . each bird a vital part of beauty that can still remain
Despite man's devastation of this lovely planet they call Earth.
They think themselves above regard for life, for death, for yearly birth
Of precious humble creatures who are emblems of creation's plan
But constantly must suffer from destruction of their home by man.

Familiar cliffs now lie ahead. The air smells strange. I cannot breathe
The freshness of the springtime air. I must fly on. I cannot leave
Until my yearly mission ends, yet this time as we reach the shore
Our world has changed. It's sinister. The beach is black, the
                                                    waves don't roar
But tumble sluggishly . . . and now the heaving sea is brown, not green.
The air smells foul. Our ancient home is now an unfamiliar scene.
But I am hungry. I must feed. The flight was long. I'm weary now.
A simple meal will strengthen me to find my mate, renew our vow
Of carrying on our gentle race to fill the air with shining wings . . .
An emblem of renewal that each turning year forever brings.

Something is wrong. My home, the sea, is now a different element:
No fish below, no air above. My eyes are filmed, my strength is spent.
I can no longer lift my wings. The waves are rolling me ashore
In tides of black and stinking filth. I'm poisoned, dying.
          What's it for?
Lord of the Birds, have mercy now. My longed-for home is out of reach.
Release my spirit, ease my pain! I die on this once friendly beach.

Audrey Forbes-Handley

THE PROMISED LAND

God spoke to Moses one fine day
And said 'Now you will lead the way
Across the desert with all my people
        Into the *promised land.*

You will take all the cattle
The goats and the sheep
The Egyptians will give you many things to keep
        And take. To the *promised land.*

And Pharaoh will chase you
With chariots and men,
To take you as slaves to Egypt again
        Away from the *promised land.*

You will come to the seaside
And there you will stop
While the army comes after you, clippety clop,
And the people will cry 'What shall we do?'
        'Oh, where is the *promised land?'*

And then I will show *my might* and *my power*
I'll roll the sea back till it stands like a tower,
On this side and that side and you will march through
And Pharaoh will follow for he thinks he's trapped you,

Then I, the *great* and *almighty God*
Will look down upon him and his army of men
And the waters will roll down in strength upon them.
And you will go on, being guided by Me
Till you come to the *Promised land.'*

N Stoddart

MANHUNT

There once was a lady named Carrie
Who decided that she ought to marry
But to keep to her plan
She needed a man
And her age meant that she must not tarry.

The first man she dated was Roger
Who turned out to be an old codger
He planned all his days
Was so set in his ways
She wouldn't have him as a lodger.

She then became friendly with Terry
Who liked to be jolly and merry
But too fond of his beer
Became her great fear
And marriage quite unnecessary.

One night at a club she met Ray
But then he confessed he was gay
What a pity she said
You will not share my bed
Otherwise I would like you to stay.

An aunt introduced her to Dennis
But he was an absolute menace
His service he told
Was incredibly bold
And then he went off to play tennis.

At last came the day she met John
Who could certainly turn her on
He was witty and funny
Had plenty of money
And a fabulous home in Saigon.

Eleanor West

FANTASY WORLD

The rides become faster, higher and wetter all the time
the sheer excitement and sometimes apprehension
at trying out a new experience for the first time
the look on faces after the exhilaration really says it all
expressions of pleasure and some of sheer fright
just adds to the atmosphere of the place
there is entertainment with bands performing live on stage
and 3D cinemas with all sorts that seem to jump out at you
cable-cars that reach high above the tree line
to view the spectacular scenery below
and the usual sights of hot dog and refreshment stands
are there as well
and those machines where you can win a toy
but the mechanical claw never grips properly
and slips off most of the time
and when old rides don't attract the crowds
there's always new ideas to take their place
it's like a fantasy world for any age to enjoy
I like the pictures taken
showing the true reaction on rides
that have been tried
and there's always other momentos to keep
for reminders of the day.
at the end of the day the rides close down,
the park seems like a ghost town
so chilling with the silence, everything is still
until the following day
when it all comes back to life again

Vanessa Salt

ANOTHER LONELY NIGHT

My husband is a pie and mash man
And pies I can make till the cows come home,
But potatoes my garden will not grow
And carrots my poor back will not sow.

'Darling, do you fancy a drink?' my beloved once
Said after a fit of passion one Saturday night,
'Yes please,' I replied 'a brandy and lime'
'Make mine a double,' he muttered as he turned
Off the light!

I suggested a holiday, just the two of us, alone
In an intimate setting, way off the beaten track,
He got sun stroke, diarrhoea and food poisoning
And spent the whole week flat on his back!

'Children would be nice dear,' I softly whispered
One night, parading around in black suspenders and tights,
'Who would look after the dog,' he moaned,
'When you're nursing a child and I'm not at home!'

The king of romance my husband isn't
But what he lacks in emotion he makes up for in sense,
But the sound of tiny feet would be rather nice
Instead of the thud of his football hitting the fence.

He's slowly improving and he has enrolled in a class
The only trouble is, he's out every night,
I'm sick of him drooling over love sick birds
Still, at least it's the yellow feathered type!

Selena Pearce

I ONCE NEW A LIBERAL LADY

I once knew a Liberal Lady
  who never said *no* or *maybe,*
But always said *yes*
  To all and any request
So generous and agreeable
  was she,
That when propositioned
  by a *monk*
Who asked if she
  would do it for free,
Replied but of course
  I would not think
of charging the clergy
  So now she's the cleaner
of the local *monastery* . . .

Gerald Aldred Judge

SPRING AND THE PANORAMA

It was just another day
But today spring was in the air.
The view from the panorama was beautiful.
It was filled with the winds of time.
And all the hunting cries of the sea
Under the shining moon.
It's such a beautiful place.
A place where lambs leap and heather grows.
I yearn for that beautiful place.
I remember it as I lie sleeping.
And the memories that it holds.
I dream that I will return to the beautiful place
Under the shining moon.

J L Balchim

SOME YOU WIN

He was born into a Polish occupied Ukraine,
    Coped with that.
Then the Stalinist Russians came,
Took the farm and sent his parents to Siberia,
    Coped with that.
Then the Germans came,
Put him into their army,
    Coped with that.
Then he came to Britain,
Learned English, found work,
Married, had a son,
Became a British citizen,
    Coped with that.
Then he was sacked, near to retiring,
After sixteen years with a firm,
    Coped with that.
Now he may have rectal cancer.
I hope my love copes with that.

Teresa Kowal

NEW VISION OF LOVE

Sheila is a small petite lady
Dressed so smart in red and white
Sparkling eyes twinkled brightly
from such a rosy face!
Small gifts and perfume greeted
A person lost in thought
Turning isolation into growing
Passion
Love turned its grateful corner.

D Evans

THE BORROWED CAT

Now Arthur was a kitten cat
On loan to us you see
And Arthur's favourite trick
Was to climb right up a tree
He climbed and climbed and climbed up
To the very top
But when it came to getting down
He came to a full stop
He stayed up there and cried and cried
Till mummy came to see
To get him down she had to climb
That very Arthur's tree
So daddy bought a furry mouse
Which Arthur thought was fun
He hid it up and down the house
And after it did run
We thought the mouse would be quite safe
But Arthur did not fail
While we were out one night
He ate the mouse's tail
The cat next door was Tigger
Arthur's bosom pal
They even went next door but one
To visit Auntie Val
Every day they played out
And frolicked in the sun
For Tigger's life and Arthur's
Had only just begun
The years have flown but he's still with me
He thinks our house is best you see.

Jean Thornton

COLOURS

Should have known better but I couldn't leave the colours of my dream,
One was cream and the others were true,
But I can't remember seeing blue.
Green began to mix with yellow,
Which turned into a nice young fellow.
Purple disappeared to find red,
But I believe it was truly dead.
Orange went a funny shade of pale,
Because it couldn't resist to tell a tale.
Black took it upon itself to get rid of white,
Just in case they had a fight.
And brown decided to hide grey,
But now they'll all have to pay,
Cause I have drifted
           Far-away

Titarnia Payton Lubbuck

UPROOTED

New experiences can be both daunting and exciting,
whether it be . . . moving or a job, both enlightening.
Scary, a wave in the calm, soothing sea
or, as harmonious as the buzz of a honey bee.
As a child we moved to a house so huge,
a castle it seemed with a garden of green and rouge.
Room to room, I walked in despair . . .
a bungalow . . . flat . . . no stairs!
No more sliding down, with a bump and a fall,
but no more running to the top when I hear someone call.
I decided that this house was acceptable and welcoming . . .
as my fun, adventure and escapades were just commencing.

Adele E McCafferty

MOTHER'S LOVE

If I should die before I wake,
Here's one or two notes for you to take.
Although I'll watch from up above,
I want my children smothered in love.
Clean white socks and lots of treats,
But not forgetting healthy eats.
I want them always to laugh and play
And never worry come what may.
Teach them to love and how to care,
To look after each other and learn to share.
Tell them how special and clever they are,
And let them know you're never too far.
Knowing how your love shines will make them strong too
So they will never be afraid to venture anew,
For being a good parent is not an easy task
Never knowing what questions will next be asked
So float between clouds of patience and love,
Then you and our children should fit like a glove,
I like to think no-one can raise them like I,
But I know you would more than really try.
And last but not least you my dear,
Our love tie's so strong I will always be near.

Tracy Bell-Young

SONG OF THE FAIRIES

It was early in the morning,
Before I got out of bed;
When behold! I heard some fairies:
Singing the song of the dead

I rushed out to the window;
Low what did I see:
Only a chain of fairies
Burying a dead bumble-bee

42

One fairy a censer swung
To the rhythm of their song;
A solemn chant, te-deum was rung,
As they slowly walked along.

On fragrant flowers the bumble-bee was laid;
The fairies sang te-deum, te-deum, then prayed;
Gathered in a fairy-ring, they prayed from five to seven;
God have mercy on the bee, and take his soul to heaven.

Edward Holmes

GROWING-UP

When you were young you had many a fall
Climbing the stairs - or chasing a ball
On your skateboard, or riding your bike
There were many times you gave me a fright

But now that you've grown up that much more
Your choice of activities is making me poor
The moods you get are driving me mad
One minute I'm happy, the next I'm sad

They say that the teens is a terrible time
You're there now - and all you do is whine
If this is what's coming, I expect
We will both have cause for much regret

I didn't become an adult without being a child
And yes you're right - I drove my mum wild
It's the same for us all, don't you see
We tug at the chains - we want to be free

Knowing these feelings, and loving you so
The time has now come - I'm letting you go.

Christine Thain

WHO KNOWS

Why do they do these things?
Don't they realise the hurt
We go through,
We sit and watch,
As their lives turn to dust,
But we can do nothing.
Helplessly we wonder,
Whether we can do a thing,
But there is no answer.
Our problem is unsolvable,
The choice is theirs,
I guess,
It still doesn't help us though,
We have to sort out the mess.
The terror in their eyes,
Is so bright and so intense,
As the routine procedure is about to commence.
They say it gives them pleasure,
But all I see is pain,
They do it to be clever,
And to keep themselves together,
All I can see is destruction and fear,
Which gradually pulls them apart,
Until there is nothing left but dust.

Rebecca Jones

AUTUMN

Crunch crunch
Go the leaves
under my feet.
Shine shine
goes the golden sun.
Bang bang
Go the crunchy conkers.

Bang bang
Go the exploding fireworks.
Squeak squeak
Go the hibernating squirrels.
Trick or treat
Say the kids on Hallowe'en.
These are the things that tell me it's winter time.

Jon Welch (11)

GIRL IN THE PICTURE

Glints the hair from rays of sun
Cascading tresses in curls of fun
Nestling the elfin featured jaw
Tousled locks like flaxen straw.

The distant gaze of gimlet blue eye
Peeking under its golden sky
Vanishing to a faraway point
What's in your mind, what's in your thought.

In matter of fact pose you sit unaware
Pert lips apart embracing the air
Your body swathed in Hawaiian leisure
Oblivious to all your womanly pleasure.

Bermuda jeans that subtly hug
Around silky thighs they fit so snug
Legs dipped and crossed so nonchalantly tease
Your feminine sexuality displayed with ease.

My hands move quickly putting paint on paper
Working to capture your grace and favour
Like a photograph's image captures moments in time
Girl in my picture, you are truly divine.

Michael Gardner

THE WORLD AT MY FEET

Two years ago this May
I started a part-time job.
Looking after the elderly,
A job close to my heart.

The staff are lovely and friendly,
giving a homely atmosphere.
We're on first name terms
with everyone
even giving sad residents
a hug and kiss to cheer.

The friends I have made
they're both young and old,
have given me an outlet
for my happiness to unfold.

Gwyneth John

MOTHER'S LOVE

A mother's love is pure of heart
Of whose children she hates to part
She knows the way of right and wrong
Many a night she worked so hard and long
To help to clothe and feed us is a must
Selflessness not of nature she we trust
She washes irons just to keep us all clean
Why should we fight and be so mean
A day of work we always think so hard to do
But mother's trust will always see us through
Think that when we call and hurt our mothers
A friend to us and many, many others
If she was absent from our lives and heart
Our lifelong friend and special confidant.

Yvonne Stevens

NAUGHTY AUNT MAUDE

My Auntie Maude came home to see us
To avoid the police so she said
She was pretty and naughty
perhaps around forty
plump kissable lips of bright red.

Her back slapping laugh was so joyful,
Her scent called Exotic Dreams,
She jumped and she jiggled
Wobbled and wiggled
Uttering delicious ear-splitting screams.

She played blind man's buff with us children.
Sucked rabbit bits through her gold teeth.
Held dimpled arms high
Well as high as her thigh
Kissed all she could catch underneath.

She drank twenty three Port and lemons
Pulled faces, sang very rude songs
The cops came at four
She breezed through the door
Bye bye lovies won't be too long.

My naughty Aunt Maude went to prison.
Dad couldn't afford the ten quid
I was glad that she came,
Life isn't the same,
But I never found out what she did.

Irene Ison

HUMBUGS AND PEPPERMINT PIPE

Martin Matthew and Mark
Dressed up just for a lark,
They put on red noses
And shoes with no toeses,
Which made all the dogs want to bark.
      However
Uncle Freddie became rather ill
When he came to look at the will,
'Dear me,' he then said,
I'll go, up to bed,
Instead he climbed up the hill.
      Now
Mr Roly had very big feet,
Mr Poly's were plates of meat,
So whenever they met
Near a house that was let,
They'd trip over there in the street.
      You see
Sal's nonsense rhymes are such fun,
She makes them up on a run.
Singing Hi-fiddley-dee,
It's now time for tea,
There's a big chocolate cake and a bun.

Sally Crook-Ford

NORTHERN WINTER

Swallows
Are gone now.
Together they soar,
Innately certain
That, together,
They must seek
A warmer shore.

Now
Telegraph wires
Are bare.
Peace trembles
In the changing air,
Alone, unsure,
Begging togetherness.

Ann Stewart

WHERE'S GEM'S JERSEY

Oh where's Gem's jersey
Oh tell me have you seen,
Oh I just need to wash it
It's needing a clean.

She wore it to the cinema
She wore it to the fair,
She took it off at grandma's
But now it isn't there.

I just cannot understand where it has gone
It can't be far,
No let me think oh yes that's it
She left it in the car.

Now I've got to find this jersey
'Cause it's getting rather late,
I really have to find it
I'm getting in a state.

Now this problem's like a rhyme,
It could even be a song,
Oh no you won't believe me
I can see she's got it on.

Jean Skates

UNTITLED

Sweet and kind,
thoughtful mind,
you share your stuff,
and care enough
helpful and sweet
buy good things to eat,
Lovely and caring,
You're always sharing your
secrets with me.

Carly Evans (9)

SPIRITUAL HEALING

There's a ray that burns so bright
Turns all darkness into light
A force that's directed from above
The divine inspiration fed by love

How can we achieve this state
Who will show how to open the gate
Service to God will show the way
Hard work and learning will guide the ray

All are worthy of this trust
Obedience and purity is a must
Teachers can help reach your goal .
You must be at one with your soul

What is this gift that God gives free
Open your eyes and you will see
Clear your mind, achieve that loving feeling
Then you're granted the power of spiritual healing

Eric Motson

NATURE'S WAY

Darkness descends, like mantle or cloak,
Falling and pushing down under oak,
Animals, creatures, come out to play,
Knowing they have only, until the day,
To forage and dig, or roll in the corn,
Safe in the dark, but only till morn,
But, not safe from the hunter on top of the hill,
The fox lies awaiting, the rabbits to kill,
The cats kill the birds, or even the rats,
Swiftly mice scurry, avoiding the bats.
Cruel think some, but nature must work,
Creating a circle, not such a strange quirk.
Before darkness rises, like lifting a valance
Mother Nature works hard, keeping the balance.
True to the circle, she greets every dawn
As with pain, and with effort come cries of new born.

Margaret Laws

IF ONLY

If only I could be reborn
And live my life again
I'd spread more happiness
And cause a lot less pain

I've made some terrible mistakes
And for them I have paid
And I've been filled with self-reproach
When on the past I've preyed

But then on second thoughts we know
Ourselves we must forgive
And make the best of the few years
That we have left to live.

Joan Knapman

SHADOWS FROM THE HEART

The tiny seed greweth from the ground
Revealed the petals, sweet smells of sound
Shadows of light shadows of gold
Gave back the glory, brought back the bold
Hidden traces of immaculate love
Blended the person who weareth the glove

The speak of Venus's words of true
Consuming the vision struggling with night
The rush of wings *cast wide*
Mastered the great love, colours of blue

The wisdom of angels the break of a kiss
Hidden waters traced of one's hate
Fetched forth the birth of tender bliss,

Once was time sureth of wind
Come forth dazzled look
The sighting elements of a wandering star
Scattered the love, so near so far

Look yonder sad soul, the flight of a dove
Great circling of clouds
Reach down on pastures green
Streams that glitter, the essence of love . . .

Mark Peter Evans

T

My friend's name is . . . I won't say,
'Cause he's shy, modest that way.
But in all the world I know
He is good . . . generously so!

> Friends who talk, and mates who touch,
> Are a help, they give you much;
> But my pal - who I can't say -
> Gave me cash and saved the day!

There are those (and they are teem)
Who would judge this poem, deem
It unworthy of a soul . . .
Yet in same breath praise gold's role!

> Let me answer from the heart:
> Ain't no soul when belly smart!
> So, if you got friends like 'T' -
> Money where mouth is . . . talk is free!

James Parry

BLACK STUFF

Face of black like the dead of night
Sweat rolling down making zebra stripes
Coughing, choking, from the density of dust
Picking, shovelling at the black diamond crust
Roof a-cracking, roof a-falling,
Time to move from this blackened tomb
Not much time must get out quick
Or we might be buried alive
Warning over, still a-crouching, back to work
In this black diamond mine.

C R Wilkinson

53

A FRIEND FROM LONDON

A friend to share realities with,
Who walks on mountains high,
Whose spirit of adventure is like mine,
Who suffers sweatened brow akin,
Overcoming nature's craft with ankle sprained,
Camping wild on Garsdale's ice carved wilderness,
Tumbling down lakeland becks in freshened sparkle,
No rumblings from our wives!
Clambering over mist filled Crinkle Crags,
Scrambling the Lords Rake and West Wall Traverse,
Snug under Scaefells' crest,
Returning past Waast waters' bruised slopes,
To enjoy Ambleside's best fish and chips!
Resting in these moments now,
A friendship fostered in these fells,
Stirred perspective into London life,
Continued into family life,
Where hour may pass it remains the same!
A rock of encouragement and support.
Withstanding earthly sprays and splash,
Out of sight but ignited by an eternal light!

Martin Norman

ELLIOT

I know a young man who feels ten feet tall
He rides a bike tho' not to school
With bated breath I wait for his call
I'm sure he is aiming for the brick wall.
Daringly he turns his head
Watch me Nan I can go very fast
Now I've no stabilisers at last.

His hands don't quite reach the brake
The foot will do, never mind the hole in the shoe.
Thank goodness he can now use his brakes.
Oh no! Now he has a bump on his head,
Try using your brakes instead.

Barbara Ling

TIME TO WAKE UP

Tired to wake up tired to look around
Tired to know all is OK
I'm bored again
My doctors tell me to take another
Tablet
I'm still bored that's all doctors seem to do
I don't know what or why I take them
I feel bad and unwell in my self
I pray and ask for help
I want to know why I'm like I am
These people talk and laugh
Is it my paranoia or are they
Really looking funny at me
I look around and have no direction
To go when I go to bed I say
Wishing for dreams to come true
When will I get married?
I wonder if it's staying in a dream
Too tired to wake up
But wake up is what I need.

Roger Brooks

MY COMPUTER MAN

I went to see him to see him to find out if he was OK
but we kissed and rekindled dormant love, that Saturday.
He decided that he would take on dogs and goldfish too,
but mostly he said, two young girls and my darling you.

His wife, my friend had walked out on him a week before,
now the chance of happiness for all of us, an open door.
He held the key, he unlocked and our hearts opened wide,
he had love for us all and gentleness and so much pride.

We had a lot of adjusting to do, he to me, and me to him,
I had to learn of this scary temper, that was pretty grim.
He had had it too easy for too long, never had to care,
and then he had me to argue back and also me to share.

Life has not always been easy, we have often found out,
he and the girls have been to hell and back without doubt.
But each understands more and are learning and he cares,
he loves them as his own and their lives he always shares.

He has found out my hang-ups, my worries doubts and fears,
put right what he could, cuddled me and wiped away tears.
My man works with computers, head of IT and he's good,
his knowledge is vast, and he would always help if he could.

I will never forget what and how much that he gave up for me,
always I will care and love him, my reason for being is he.
No one can ever take away the memories or moments of passion,
or split us up, we are as one, our love is always in fashion.

He even had to choose between his kin and me and he chose me,
I feel humble but also sad for they lost him then you see.
My man's hobby is computers and he gave that up for me too,
the song says I would die for him, yes my computer man, you.

Jill Bramhall

56

REFLECTIONS

In the September of life, I think of the past,
Where did time go, it went too fast,
Memories of my childhood years,
The joys, the sorrows, the laughter and tears,
Times change through the years, when you are over the hill,
That's progress, nothing stands still
You have done your work, now it's the turn,
Of younger people, their living to earn,
As you sit and reflect on days gone by
Your life work finished and retirement nigh,
You wonder sometimes what life's all about,
When you have faith, there is no room for doubt.

Ruby Ingham

JUST ANOTHER INNOCENT

Deepest sorrow, darkest anger,
Both emotions grip my heart,
Followed by my anguished plea,
'God - let this day restart!'

It's happening so frequently,
I read the papers every day,
Am moved by childish innocence,
At young life snatched away.

Most parents love their children,
Build a future they hope to share,
Dreams crushed by some crazed misfit,
The world should take more care!

Christine Hulme

MOTHER GAZELLE

Mother Gazelle prepares for the birth of her new-born
It arrives into the world, a healthy young fawn
She licks it often and leaves it odourless
If predators are near it must remain motionless.

Mother moves it to a sanctuary place
And nestles it in the tall grass
New-borns are easy prey if hunters pass
She will be alert for it from dusk till dawn
She moves slowly now to collect her fawn.

It is now two weeks since the fawn's arrival
It can stand, jump, and play and has a better
chance of survival
Mother lets it have a quick suckle, as there are
targets even standing still
She begins to show her fawn her hunting skills,

The bond begins with the fawn and its mother
They share a lush meal with each other
The best luxury in life for the fawn is having
Mother's protection from dusk till dawn.

Rose Bell

MY EVER EXPANDING WAISTLINE

7 months pregnant and growing bigger
I'm really starting to show.
I feel like the enormous turnip,
I think I'll soon explode.

It started as a little bump
all cute and harmless really,
but spread like wildflower
I've put on 2 stones nearly.

The clothes I had are all too small
now stretched and out of shape.
I haven't seen my toes for months
with all this extra weight!

But time will come and it will be gone
this bump I've grown quite fond of,
replaced by a cute, pink, cuddly thing
I can protect and smother with love.

Deborah Durbin

CHILDREN

Why do children always do
The opposite that you want them to?
'Close the door' you've often cried
What do they do? Open it wide

'Come here now, get your hair brushed!'
They'll stay where they are - there's no rush
'Go to bed now' - they'll want to stay up
'Bring me a plate' - they'll bring you a cup

'Don't run kids, just have a nice walk'
Why do we even bother to talk?
'Don't kick the ball at the window son'
'But I have to Dad, it's brilliant fun!'

It's pouring with rain - they want to go out
The sunshine's blazing and you have to shout
And surgically remove them from the couch
'That really hurt Mum, ouch!'

The conclusion that I've come to over the years
After oceans of blood, sweat and tears
If there's something that you want them to do
Ask them not to, and they'll do it for you!

June Mackillop

WHO TOOK THE RAIN (SUMMER 95)

The lush green grass is now a yellow mass
Even the cows complain, who took the rain?
Normally we say, rain rain go away, but we need some
Today
Who took the rain
Garden flowers parched in the sun, usually a colourful
Display.
But not today, who took the rain
Farmers' crops for selling in the shops, they're dying too
What will they do
Who took the rain
Irrigation I remember that, long ago forgotten now
The crops turn rotten
Who took the rain
It's too hot to walk about, sit in the sun and shout
Why have we got a drought
Who took the rain
We are an island in the sun water all around
But none for the ground
Who took the rain
Never prepared for flood, never prepared for drought
The water board try and explain what it's all about
Reservoirs all gone dry, no *wet stuff* in the sky
I'll never again complain,
When it starts to rain
So! Who took the rain?
Something must be done, 'cos this goes on and on
It must not happen again
It *never* happens in Spain
Who took the rain?

Irene Witté

SCENES OF SPLENDOUR

Walk in the splendour of the dales and hills
where purple hues mingle amidst awesome majestic peaks,
slowly ascending crags stretch up towards the clouds
enshrouded in their misty capes, disappearing from sight.
Walk through the fells to foothills of the tarns
listen as the woodpecker calls out across the vale,
where bracken crispy brown crackles under foot
while meandering streams and riverlets
cascade in gentle fall.

Stroll beneath the canopy of leaning anvil tops
as stunted trees to battle, against ever rising winds,
who pays a season's call, bringing a dampened chill.
Those ever climbing gradients soon reach the deep dark pools
and mossy paths get wider in the valley between the rocks,
while mountains' mirror images border like a frieze
such graphic scenes are illustrated, no old master could create.

A labyrinth of lines trace out across the bowl
while winding tracks entice
to seek distant views beyond.
Enveloped in this beauty, of never tiring scenes
breathless not from walking, but what it is we see,
and standing in its midst, we wonder at it all
for such a tranquil setting
stills the roaring beast.

Helen J Lewis

61

MY HEART WILL FEEL

I stand in a field
and let my mind go astray
as a love has begun
in my heart on this day.

When I walked in the room
my heart felt such lust
like a bubble
unbound not to bust,
pure sweet emotion
flowed through my veins
no other woman have I ever loved the same.
The passion and desire
entered my soul
and my spirit began to chill,
and to this day
I hope and pray
that woman my heart will feel.

I P Smyth

BEREAVEMENT

Lift your hand gently and turn out the sun
The short day is over, long night begun
The butterfly broken, frail was its wing
The song-bird is silent, no more to sing
The last leaf fallen, to time all succumb
Lift your hand gently and turn out the sun
Your time was my time, now your time is done
The short pain is over, long peace begun
Now you have left me my living is done
Lift your hand gently and turn out the sun.

Lily Duncan

INSOMNIA

What can I do when I lie in bed - and the pain starts again and thuds
through my head?
My hands start to swell, throbbing with pain, my elbows, my knees,
they are the same!
I struggle to sit and reach for a drink, to take some more pills, (to cure
it I think).

The lid on the bottle, it's on too tight, I can't open the thing on my own
in the night.
A packet I'll try that you push the pills through, but that's just as bad.
- Oh! I'll go to the loo.
Now I'm stuck in my bed, can't stand on the floor, can't shuffle about
or get to the door.

This is no fun, helpless like child. I'd moan to the Doc, but he'd say
'It's just mild.'
I'm feeling fed up - if only you knew, how useless I feel, when I'm
having a *Do*.
Go back to sleep 'cos there's no more to say? No - I'll lie here awake
and wait for the day.

Soon daybreak will come - a new day will start. I'll smile at the world
and try to act smart.
The World sees the smile and thinks I'm all right. No sign of the pain
that's there in the night.
So if you see that smile and say 'How are you?' Don't believe what I say -
You haven't a clue!

Drew Michaels

63

A GLIMPSE OF AN EVACUEE'S LIFE

Hello it's me an evacuee,
I'm just dropping by for a tasty tea,
I'm in the countryside isn't that fab,
There aren't any cars I suppose that's
not bad,
The cows go moo all day long,
I wish they would stop singing their
song,
Mrs May is kind and helpful,
I'm sure she thinks I'm a bit of a
handful,
She makes lovely teas and is very
jolly,
And when it rains she forgets her
brolly,
There are other children in the house,
I don't like the girl she's afraid of a
mouse,
I suppose the two boys are better than
her,
But they pretend they're cats so they
always purr,
I suppose the country's OK but I don't
want to live here every day.

Hajar Javaheri (10)

MY GARDEN

Once again spring has arrived
The trees long bare in leaf again
Ice, frost, and snow have disappeared
Now comes the gentle rain.

Crocus, snowdrops, daffodils
Were such a lovely sight
Magnolia now in blossom
A splendid waxen white,

Two greater spotted woodpeckers
Arrive to feed each day
They love to eat the fat and nuts
And give a wonderful display.

Squirrels, hedgehogs, rabbits
Stoats and weasels too
Come to visit the garden
Damp and fresh with dew.

There's babies in the black teapot
Where Mrs Robin rest
And in a box near to the door
A bluetit builds her nest.

A blackbird sits high on a bough
Singing his cheerful song
The starlings love their daily bath
Owls screech all night long.

Where is this lovely place you ask
With flowers of every hue
Where birds and animals abound
My garden is the view.

Freda Nobes

BRING BACK THE CAT

My brother he was seven
When I was only five
He was always bossing me
But I didn't run and hide
Boxing gloves for Christmas
Later on in life
No drugs or batons
Or car to run away
I resolutely stood my ground
In the ring you have to stay
He's not quite so bossy now
And I know the reason why
When it's him that's getting punched around
Your ego's not the same
Especially
When it's you that feels the pain

F Oldfield

MY IMPULSIVE HUSBAND

That was his way, the day we wed,
He wouldn't change, despite what I'd said.
He'd always utter 'I want one of those.'
The very next day I'd see it parked in the road.
I've seen them come, I've seen them go,
Zephyrs, Chevvies, all for show.
Jaguars, Lincolns, yes, the lot,
It's just to say, 'Look what I've got.'
I shouldn't complain, he works hard for a living,
It's just, I wish, one day he'd give in.

Jackie White

WILL THEY NEVER HEED

Standing in a field in the middle of nowhere
Hearing whispered voices but there's no one there
Alone in the middle of no man's land
Earthy smells on the midnight air.

Soft pressures felt against my body
Urging me to something I know not what
I hear English spoken, German and French
Almost inaudible, I almost hear not.

I see not but I hear much louder
Faint forms slowly beginning to rise
Dressed in tunics, some in khaki
Stumbling forward with plaintive cries.

'Be not afraid' they seem to whisper
'But, carry our message to the world'
'That now seems to be on the brink of disaster'
'Let the flags of hate never be unfurled.'

Am I dreaming? I seem too much aware
Figures now fading into the ground
They are muttering over and over again
'Try again for peace, let it be new found.'

I left this field at the dawn's light
On high ground I saw fluttering standards
Around me mushroomed white tombstones
I departed from this field in Flanders.

R Nield

LOOKING FOR LOVE

Why is true love, so hard to find?
Yet looking for this, we spend most of our time?
And when we find someone to date
He's already found, his perfect mate

True love is something, that I'm looking for
And not the false kind, because I want more
A close friend, a buddy, or mate
Surely it can't, be just left to fate.

Whenever I think, I've really found love
Someone up there, starts laughing above
It always ends, with so much pain,
It makes me wonder, why I bother again.

But to feel the strength, of your warm embrace
And to look at that smile, upon your face
To feel that kiss, that sends shivers inside
Makes up for the times, I've sat and cried.

So to keep on looking, that's what I'll have to do
To find this love, so perfect and true
I hope, I won't have to wait forever
For true love and I to get together.

Ann Harford

SPRING

Spring is when the buds appear
On all the shrubs and trees
And sunshine breaking through the clouds
To wake up the birds and bees

The lambs are skipping in the fields
Young rabbits scamper round
While fox and badger keep their young
Hidden underground

The daffodils are all in bloom
Wallflower and stock as well
The fields are full of fresh green grass
And bluebells in the dell

The hedgerows all look lovely
With foxgloves growing high
The gorse and pink campion mix
With bees and dragonfly

Camilla Clemens

WHEN SHADOWS FALL

Upon the pillows of the night
In dreamy moods of sleep,
Requited passions of the day
Succumb to nature's keep.

As shadows drift by silently
To curtain woodland glades,
Enhanced the evening's solitude,
By tranquil serenades.

Soft perfumed breezes fume the air
All is quiet and still,
The volumed sounds of *nature's* heart
Soothed by night's overspill.

Upon the pillows of the night
Soft dewy tears now fall, as,
The sunset's silent beauty fades
And *nightingales* enthral.

Malcolm Wilson Bucknall

LIFE IS TOO SHORT

Why must I sigh, why must I dream,
New paths are before me, with so much to be seen,
I look through my window
            as the raindrops fall.
My coat I'll now gather, to walk down
                that grey hall,
Life is too short I now understand,
The badness and evil are now off my hands.
The long lonely years, I've stared
           at grey walls,
But now I'll walk free, as winter just falls.
My past now behind me, these years
             gone waste,
My past now behind me, these years gone waste,
As shut away in hell again,
          I hope I'll never taste.

Rita Andain

SPRING

I cannot wait for spring to come
With all its pretty posies
The crocus, and the daffodil
The snowdrops, and primroses
The birds that sing
The little lambs
Are part of this time too
I cannot wait for this to come
The start of all things new.

O Stringer

70

MY HEART AND SOUL HAS BEEN TORN AWAY

My heart and soul has collapsed,
I can't breathe anymore,
I feel as if I am being enclosed in a tiny space,
There's nowhere to breathe,
And now time to leave,
I feel as if someone somewhere is tearing away at my heart and soul,
And stretching it at great speed and length,
My mouth is fastened up tightly,
As I am concealed in this tiny little space,
I have had my heart broken once too often,
The pain had been too much for me that time,
But the pain had never ever hurt as much as it does now,
The pain is growing and growing,
It's growing with great strength and length,
I feel so much pain and suffering inside me,
My heart's pounding over and over again,
The pain will be here forever more,
Coming closer and closer,
Beginning to kill me,
I can feel my neck getting tighter and tighter,
I've been enclosed in such a tiny space and I'm all alone,
No-one to help me,
And no-one to talk to,
Slowly but surely I am beginning to die.
I'm swivelling up into pieces,
I'm in a state of shock,
In almost an instant,
I begin to feel the pain getting stronger and stronger,
And suddenly my eyes close and fasten up tightly,
My soul has risen and I am free at last.

Aliya Hanif

STREET BEGGAR

That withering look you give me
Speaks volumes as you hurry on by
Crossing the road in avoidance
Thinking to yourself, he just doesn't try.

Get a job, go to work, get a life
He only wants money for booze.
My very presence offends you.
But you, what have you got to lose.

In your comfortable world of plenty
A warm bed and a family that cares
Weekend barbecues, and Sunday roasts
Not forgetting, your Sunday prayers.

Christian, take a long hard look
Let me tell you what you don't see
I'm a person with no future
Desperate to retain some dignity.

I too had a mother and father
Father was too fond of his beer
Mother was too weak to protect me
And the beatings became too severe.

At fifteen I just ran away
But I don't ask for your sympathy.
Just a little understanding
And some change for a cup of tea.

Jenny Whitehead

NEVER GIVE UP

Never give up, no matter what comes along,
For you will see a bit later you'll
              be guided where you belong.
Everything is for a reason, the good
                  and the bad.
For without all the struggles, you
              won't appreciate the glad.
So when people say we get
              older and wiser it's true.
For we all learn from our mistakes
           as we are passing through.
And as we grow in wisdom, and
              learn to take things in our stride,
We find that things get easier
              than when we were young inside.
So try to take one day at a time,
           and very soon you'll see, that
things are much better today
             than they were yesterday.

Alice Polley

AS I SLEEP, I DREAM

As I sleep, I dream and for a short moment
can escape from my gloomy world into
a world of fun, laughter and freedom,
but only for a few brief hours
until another break of day
Comes in to my gloomy world of
This bullied child that's now
a prisoner until the night comes again
and I then can return to my dream-world
of happiness.

Michael Spittles

ODE TO OLE GINGER

Froggy, froggy, moist and slight,
Prince of pools
And least in *sight.*
Who can claim,
Oh! Handsome guy
To top *you*
As the gals hop by.
Mister in your lurid coat,
Bright of hue
You've got the vote.
And the view
Of all your clan . . .
The *hippiest* frog
In all the land.
And you're kinder:
Thousands! Throng
Cried,
'LookitmeDa'
Soo - biiig . . . 'n' strong.'
Then one day . . .
Sad to relate,
There lay Ginger;
Out of shape,
Lying still, and,
Without fuss.
Poor Ole Ginger
squashed
by a
bus!

Mary Kelly

PARADISE

Lord, grant me strength to wither joyfully
As blue skies turn to grey
Like the yellow leaf in autumn
When swallows fly away.
Lord, help me bear my sorrows
Then glorious I shall stand
When a better springtime cometh
In the Glory Land
Lord, bless me this I pray
When winter comes, and ice
Then open wide for me
A lasting Paradise.

David Blair

SINGLE MEN

Up at seven thirty
Out on the job
Forty hours weekly
To earn a few bob,
Can't wait for Friday
Down to the pub,
skint on a Sunday
Must get a sub,
Back to work Monday
Starting again
This is the life
of most single men
Don't get much pleasure
can't have a wife
some people say
it's a wonderful life
well it's not.

O O'Reilly

IN OUR EYE

As we grow older
We have to try.
To keep that sparkle in our eye.
Step out with a vigour
As brisk as we can.
Have a good diet
Remember the *bran*!
Early to bed and late to rise
Will keep that sparkle in our eyes.
Some gentle exercise
Taken each day
Will help keep the aches and
                    pains at bay
So take this advice,
And you will see
It's not so bad, being
                    an OAP.

Irene Hannaford

HEALTH OR WEALTH

It's nice to be healthy and wise
And wealthy as well
But we cannot all have plenty
So some are sad and empty -
Of pocket for things we need
We all do indeed
To exist we must eat,
Whether it's bread or meat
And pay our way each week
Or else we will all be weak.

A Usher

LOVED ONES LOST

It's forty four years since I lost my love -
Now re-united with our son in heaven above,
The loss I still feel - the grief still great -
'Twas a heartbreaking blow - delivered by fate,
I'll never forget their smiling face -
No-one will ever take their place,
A photo on the wall still hangs -
I gaze at it - and feel the pangs -
Of loneliness and sadness too,
Tears fill my eyes - like they often do
They live forever in my mind and heart -
Both were so young when we had to part,
Now I'm ill, old and grey -
And struggle through each weary day,
I feel their presence ever near -
I see their faces - oh so clear,
I speak to them in quiet prayer -
And feel somehow that they are there,
This comforts me - although I weep -
Then I close my eyes and try to sleep,
But sleep won't come - I turn and toss -
And live again my tragic loss,
They say time heals - but that's not so -
The pain may ease - but never goes,
From my loves I'll never sever -
They'll live within my heart forever,
With aching heart I pray and wait -
Until we meet at heaven's gate.

O M Godfrey

CONFLICT

What do you think would happen today
If all the hatred went away?
Discrimination disappeared,
Of prejudice, this world was cleared.

Would we all cope? Would we feel strange
Without the comments of deranged?
Different cultures, different races,
Different people, different places.

Would it work? What do you think?
People living on the brink
Of starting wars; of making peace.
But would all fighting really cease?

Love, hate, peace, war.
This could be just like before.
All the conflict, but in silence.
I thought that this would end the violence.

The end is nigh, I am not strong.
I long to hear a joyous song;
To see doves fly, to feel the breeze;
To know the people live at ease.

But people never change. It's clear
They never know what all hold dear
To their hearts with love; to their souls with grief.
With all that's left: their own belief.

It doesn't matter where you are.
Ireland, Bosnia, afar.
The message is clear: 'It should not be,
We should live in harmony.'

Should the conflict come to end,
Would your heart begin to lend
A thoughtful wish; a tearful eye
For all of those who had to die.

To bring us peace.

Chris Throup

STILL LIFE

Respected Mr Surgeon, just look at me
and tell me what it is you see,
come feel the blood on this scalpel blade
do you like being a part of this dying trade?
Now as I lay in this darkened room
I'd much rather be in my mother's womb
snug and warm, growing bigger each day
if only unborn babies could have their say.
Well as you rest inside your bed
perhaps you might think of that baby's head
that you so mercilessly crushed for gain
all that suffering, all that pain.
Yes, and giver of life in whom we trust
am I just a victim of this woman's lust?
Would I really have got in her way
and would I really spoil her day?
Well I'd have loved you mother, with all my heart
If only you had tried to give me a start
instead of spurning me and aborting my life
would one little baby cause such strife?
I wanted to be a person, but not like you
so it's goodbye now
to the world I never knew.

S Keyes

WHAT THEN?

When mercy is a dirty word
And pity non-existent
What's to become of hope or love
Of laughter or persistence
The laughter had from over thirst
Is not a laugh that lingers
And if we don't renew our thoughts
And throw away the blinkers
No ethics in high places
And ethics when ignored
Make the very heavens tremble
And anger all the gods
Angry gods become impotent
Letting all the devils in
And devils when let loose
Make such a feast of everything
And when the feast has ended
              What then?

Rose Salter

TREES

Our trees stand tall silent and still
- above us reaching for the sky
- gently swaying in the wind.
They sigh with blossoms over me
the fallen windfalls lay scattered
like balls on the grass -
quiet the windfalls lay.

Ann Fletcher Campbell

SURPRISE, SURPRISE

The clothes are washed and ironed too,
There's such a lot I have to do.
Friends are calling round they say,
I'm sure it's right, it is today.

I've cleaned the house, the whole way through,
Windows shining, just like new.
I've cut the lawn, and trimmed the edge,
I even cut the blooming hedge!

I went to bed, so very sad
And even just a little mad.
My friends forgot to call today,
Did they break down, or lose their way?

The next day dawned, the sky was black
My limbs were aching, and my back.
I stayed indoors and moped about,
Then thought I'd turn the cupboards out.

As I sat there upon the floor
Amidst the tins and junk galore,
The cat was sick, the dog as well,
It's then I heard the front door bell.

It's probably for double glazing,
Or kids out doing school fund raising.
I tried to raise a cheerful smile
But felt like running half a mile!

My friends stood there, all looking great,
Hello dear! Hope we're not too late.
You did say 'Come to lunch today'
I thought I *had* said yesterday!

Louise Tilby

TOTALLY DEVOTED TO YOU

Stevie Stopwatch is his name
Time and motion is his game
He has panache and flair
But, he's got ginger hair

Toyed with women at this leisure
Snowboarding is his only pleasure
'Til riding Fakey one day
In a tail grab, he looked away

Three hundred and sixty degrees
Toeside, heelside over trees
He landed, applause galore
The man that I adore

Time stood still
I obeyed his will
Measured his flight of fancy
Against his Mazda and a girl named Nancy

I'm not a talker
Just a stopwatch stalker
People think that I am daft
To fancy the man on a cinnamon raft

Janette Homer

A FANTASY

You've entered *me* in a marathon?
With arthritis in both me knees,
Imagine me, in shorts of blue
You really are a tease.

Baseball cap on back to front,
Sunglasses on my nose,
I'll wear a fashion Tee Shirt
And strike an athlete's pose.

I'll join the other entrants,
With winning post in mind,
And step it out for all I'm worth
Though many miles behind.

My day of fame is over
As I slowly climb in bed,
I very nearly - done it!
Now, - I'm very nearly dead.

Betty Moir

OUR KIDS

They fill our lives with happiness
They fill our lives with joy
They fill our lives with love and fun
Our two girls and little boy
And then they have their 'off' days
When they are sick or in a mood
When they argue and they irritate
And they do not eat their food
And then you begin to wonder
'Oh no what have we done?'
We've created little monsters
Who always seem to run
Can they ever just be quiet
And just sit in one place
And why is it that no matter what
There is always a dirty face
But we really wouldn't swap them
For each day they bring such joy
And we both get so much love back
From our two girls and little boy

Kathy Staggs

A HERO'S RESTING PLACE

For them there is only one place,
One time where they may rest.
A place where they can finally yield.
Do away with flaming swords and blazing guns
For here there are no more battles to win
In a heaven they could rest.

Never again having to conquer the evil they despised
They could unfurl precious pictures of loved ones.
No longer would they fear the enemies,
Creeping in the night.
In a heaven they could rest.

Here they finish epic journeys
Away from the constant rain of sorrow
Life sent their way,
No longer dodging with speed and stealth.
In a heaven they finally rest.

Liam Quigley

DAISY

I'm a tiny flower
Daisy is my name
I live in the garden
From the earth I came
See, my golden eye
Though, I've only one
It is very bright, like the golden sun.
Every, sunny day, when I open wide,
Shaking out my petals,
You can peep inside,
Then my tiny eye, shuts up to the sun,
Then, I close up tight, when the day is done.

P Dyson

DON'T WORRY, BE HAPPY

Your mind and emotion hold the key
They're the things to set you free
Whate'er the day
Whate'er the night
Fulfil yourself with love, joy and delight

Sadness and worry
Gets you nowhere at all
Just up the wall
Whate'er the day
Whate'er the night
Fulfil yourself with love, joy and delight

With faith in Lord God
And determination
You may live a long happy life
Fulfilled with love, joy and delight
Whate'er the day
Whate'er the night
Fulfil yourself with love, joy and delight

Let people come first
Wherever you go
That's a thought
All people should show
Whate'er the day
Whate'er the night
Fulfil yourself with love, joy and delight

Paul Wilkins

LUCKY WIN FOR CHRISTMAS

December 64, Mum was feeling down, after doing washing in the tub,
Dad came home happy, after three hours down at the club.
He took one look at her. Told her to get her coat on, go to the bingo club,
Chucked onto the table thirty bob,

As she cheerfully went out the door,
Shouted, come back with the jackpot, maybe even a bit more.
That Saturday night, half past ten, no sign of her. We were getting worried,
Then, all of a sudden, in through the door, excited Mum hurried.
A bag full of fish and chips in one hand, a big envelope in the other,

Staring at her in disbelief, said, how could you afford all that mother.
She opened the envelope, emptied it onto the table,
Then, Terry and myself and Dad started counting out the notes all over the table.

Ten bob notes, £1.50 too, so many, onto the floor, some fall,
After what seemed like hours counting all that money,
There was over £350 overall.
Thinking back to that day, now seems really funny.

With all that money, all the family together,
Was the best Christmas ever (so far).

Professor Knutworthy

SILENT ANGER

When I speak why don't you answer?
Is it that you just don't care.
Is it that you are just dreaming.
Or that life is too hard to bare.

That you have spoken so many times,
Of your life's ups and downs,
Only to be continually thwarted,
By jeers and laughs and frowns.

People who listened without hearing,
Your inward silent cry,
But I can see your pain
By looking into your eye.

Let us face this pain together,
Don't face this pain alone,
We will resolve this past life together,
And remove all hate man hath sewn.

S Amphlett

DON'T TRUST TO LUCK

She wasn't superstitious
She didn't trust to luck
With old wives' tales and adages
She never had any truck

A lone magpie meant nothing
'She's only calling for her mate
Just like a man' she thought
'Always arriving late'

She ignored ladders in her path
Walked under them at will
Saw the full moon through glass
And black cats left no thrill

Friday the thirteenth
Was just another date
You never wished upon a star
Just left it to your fate

Then why did she cross her fingers
When all these things occurred
To make sure nothing happened
To make her change her word?

Yona Geddes

NOBODY LISTENS TO THE OLD I'M TOLD

Life is ticking quickly along
So much has happened, as years have gone
Now I am older something is wrong
People tell me I am not so strong
You should give up work before, too long
and let the youngsters take all the jobs on

But I don't feel old, I feel very bold
So why should I withdraw and withhold?
Nobody listens to the old I'm told!
But a conversation I can certainly hold
Some people are unfriendly, almost cold
When the age of 'me' they do unfold
And my job is soon to be bought and sold
Who will listen to me when I am old?

My skin and hair I believe have changed
But my thinning hair is not really 'mange'!
I'm not aware that I smell
My nose is normal . . . I can tell
I am really perfectly healthy . . . as well
It's a pity the young and old don't always gel
I still feel love, I still feel hate
I even enjoy a friendly date

But maintaining my health will be my wealth
And I am going to be positive about 'myself'

Susan Gerry

GOOD TIMES

Good times we've
      all had
But the veil of memory
Sometimes hides
Clouded by bad.

As we look back
On happy carefree
      days
In childhood, youth
Or years of age,
Good days in memory
      stays.

It's a wonderful thing
When we can find
So many times of
      good
Locked in the mind

R Beresford

THE TENTH LIFE

I held my darling furry one
As she was put to sleep;
We were so very close
My pussy cat and I
Sharing those last few precious moments of her life.
Expecting to feel desolate,
I felt a surge of warmth and strength instead;
'Be brave,' she said 'Go on without me,'
And that dear loving little thing
Had somehow given me
A truly special gift.

Rosa Barbary

SPRING IS IN THE AIR

As the trees whisper through the air,
Throughout the spring, and nature fair,
While birds fly, and soar through the sky, and gladly sing,
While the roving bees seem to have their fling,

From the roots of the trees, while birds perch high, swinging to a
                                                        gentle breeze
All this lovely nature, through the birds and the bees,

Now as we read this story about a certain bird who worked so hard
As he tidied cleared up a part of the ground, (in fact, he was a card)
Each leaf that was scattered, he picked up so gingerly,
With his cute little beak, which was done with ability,

Just as if he was spring cleaning,
But there was a meaning,
He cleverly put all the leaves by an edge in a small pile,
As again he tidied them all up with such pride and style

Now, when the ground was spotless, he jigged and he danced,
By then, an audience of other birds, just stared and glanced,
Still he danced and showed off, and looking around, he picked
                                                        out a partner,
There they both jigged, danced and turned around, while the audience
                                                        claps together.

After dark, and the dandy was over and tired out at last,
The other birds had enough of all the jigging, into their nests
                                    they flew, the hours were 10 long past
Oh, so weary but they all had a good time that night,
Watching the two dancers, through the clear moonlight,

What a romantic evening it was, as their wings clung together.
Nestling in the trees, whispering to one and another.

The two dancer flew off on top of the trees,
Their night scene is secret, whilst they have their spree,

While the bees still rest by the roots, it just goes to show
                                    that spring is in the air,
To even the whisper of the trees, God knows what goes on, for He
                                    is everywhere,
To the mating of animals, sheep, creatures and all that nature brings,
To all these clever birds, to the bees, and the warm air in the spring.

Jean McGovern

SORROW IN THE HEART

Don't fill your heart with sorrow as the girl walks by,
Hold your head up high, please don't follow,
The road in which she's gone will make you cry,
Instead turn and walk away,
The girl will only die,

She listens to her mind in which she obeys,
Starving herself from day to day,
Fading, fading away,

The mind of an ogre, the heart of a dove,
She means no harm,
But this girl is ill - her mind is wrong,

Painfully thin she looks - she can't see it herself as she walks along,
Turn away, don't let your heart of sorrow reach out and make you follow,
Be strong and walk along,
It's too late - she's gone too far,
Her life is ruined with no way back,
'Please turn' she calls out, 'while you can.'

Tracey Wheeler

MY REGIONAL ANTHOLOGY

Living in the south
Down the road from the capital
This is all I've known
Since I was small
But there's always good and bad
In everything we see
It's the same here and there
In every country
Life's just what you make of it
And how you do it
Later we must say we succeeded
Not blew it
Think what you've got
And what others have not
If we share with each other
Then perhaps, we can have the lot.

Stephen Butler

LIFE
(Dedicated to Mummy and Daddy)

I sat and looked out from my room,
Into the dull and rainy gloom.

The sun didn't shine,
The birds didn't sing,
No life in anything.

Until you smiled at me
And helped me see
That life was there
And you would care,
And there's life in everything.

Caroline Bunyard (10)

WEATHER OF TIME

The winds of time are blowing,
Along the shores of life.
Our soul forever growing,
As it meets problems that are rife.

But like the breezes on the shore,
Life continues for evermore.
And if we take the time to ask,
We'll be helped, with each task.
With each problem on the way,
As we journey through each day.

And when the breeze,
Guides us home,
And the leaves on the tree of life do fall,
We'll be ready, once again,
Once more to walk, down the Spirit Lane.

Hilary Ann Torrens

DREAMING

In my dreams I'd be a smuggler
I'd really look a sight
With weathered skin and twinkling eye
My bark worse than my bite
I'd sail upon the ocean
I'd feel it was my right
I'd dodge the excise men with glee
On a clear and starry night
I'd bring back silks and brandy
They'd pay dearly for my plight
I'd be so proud to ply my trade
From the back of Wight.

Linsey Brown

RDA GYMKHANA 1995

Magic fairy bridges, made for the RDA
With kippers big and Manx cats, bright painted on display

Happy smiling faces, on patient horse borne,
All waiting for the starter, with whistle, gun or horn.

Hard hats for protection, strapped firmly 'neath the chin,
Jodhpurs, and stout riding boots, smart as the newest pin.

Hopes and aspirations, shine bright in eager eyes
As trainee riders line up, to seek a glowing prize.

Proudly stand the helpers, beside each beaming charge,
Their hard work now rewarded, by well rehearsed dressage.

Clip-clop go the ponies, coats groomed until they shine,
Back and forth through obstacles, to reach the winning line.

Rosettes red and yellow, bright green and royal blue,
Proudly pinned to chests inflated, or ponies rein for you.

Juicy carrots waiting, and sugar lumps so sweet,
Gentle pats that say 'Well done' is every horses treat.

From over the hurdles, each skilful rider lands,
To merry cheers and laughter, and loudly clapping hands.

No-one is a loser, on this great day of joy.
Sweet victory is smiling, on every girl and boy.

Mr Golden Sunshine, has kept his promise true,
Beaming down on all the fun, from cloudless sky of blue.

Fizzy pop and ice cream, the order of the day,
As parents meet with old friends, to chat the time away.

Gymkhanas are super, we hold them every year,
So please drop in to see us, if you are passing near.

Bridges, kippers, fairies, form hurdles here today,
Gosh! Haven't we been busy, to make such grand display?

Violet M Corlett

JACK FROST

Cold to the touch.
I don't like Jack Frost much.
White as white.
We know Frost as such.

He's on the grass.
On the glass.
In the cars.
Here with a blast!

Beware for it's in the air.
Take care for it's everywhere.
Slip here and there.
He's bitter when near.

Dancing on the rooftops.
When temperatures drop.
Birds don't sing a lot.
But leave in flocks.

Jack Frost is old.
Colds are bold.
Offer me a summer holiday.
And I am sold!

A Sebastian

MAD COWS' DISEASE

She wasn't bad she wasn't good
But always moaning and always would
I met her out again today
She loves a chat what could I say
I had to stand I felt quite sour
I must have stood there for an hour
From start to finish all I heard
Was don't eat cow's meat they've poisoned the herd
Lay off the sausages leave off the pies
No wonder cows' arses are covered in flies
Don't buy the steak although it's now cheap
You'll find next week it's all in the sheep
And still watch out for salmonella
I really must go now and meet my fella
She crossed the road saying all this fuss
And was promptly run over by a bus.

Joyce McArdle

GOLDEN HILL (ALTON)

In the early morning sun,
Through the glass, silently,
A tractor hull-down on the hill
Leaning, lop-sided
Into the furrow it is stitching
Across the stubble,
Flying a ragged kite-tail of gulls . . .
Like a child, colouring carefully over the golden field
With a brown crayon.

G M Thorn

ENGLAND, OH MY ENGLAND!

Thousands of pounds a week they're paid to kick a ball around
How many can be trusted though, outside the football ground,
A Far East tour did little, to earn our team respect
Somehow their loutish behaviour is not what we would expect,
There was no call to celebrate though their performance did astound
That against a team of amateurs and has-beens, so few chances
                                                      had been found,
It really must have been the case they were drinking to forget
Only once, in an hour and a half they managed to find the net,
Perhaps though after such a show in that hot and humid region
They could have done us all a favour and joined the Foreign Legion.
The high jinx didn't end that night there was still more cause to fret
Worse was still to follow aboard a Cathay Pacific jet.

Yes Gazza's birthday party got a wee bit out of hand
With five thousand pounds of damage before the plane came in to land
'No-one did it! The story's false, the team was free from blame'
This is what coach Terry Venables said refuting every claim,
Despite these strong denials which seemed somewhat underhand.
The call went up for birthday boy Paul Gascoigne to be banned.
When you think how many youngsters live with a single dream
To pull on the shirt of England and play against Europe's cream,
Why should these prima donnas, act in such a way
Disgrace the flag of England and still get picked to play,
In skill they're thought this country's best, within our selection scheme
Though their off-field antics can't leave them much in the way of self-esteem.

Stephen P Jennings

ETERNAL SLEEP

All life on earth must someday - come to an end,
It's not a rehearsal, we do not come
back to do it all again.

So while we may live on God's earth below
as we do, our very best along life's way.

We sometimes may sit and think as we grow old,
of our families - and friends and of all
the memories, that may not have been told.

We as wedded partners, have shared so much,
Joys, laughter - tears, as we have gone down
through the years.

But one of us will have to die first
It's not hard to do when God has
always helped you through.

I'd leave all instruction what had to be done,
For I know my grandaughter, although
adopted you see, would always carry
my last wishes thro' for me.

And when I die, I want them that I leave behind
to save these tears - and think of all
in life we have done together - and have
love for me - so they may carry on,
until one day their life is also through.

For I no more will lift my weary head
and there will be no more
tears for them I can shed.
I'll just be a bright star; away up high
No more seasons, I will see,
as I'll leave them to my family.

And I will be comforted by God's gentle hand
hoping all will understand.
For God will take me to his promised land
I shall wait for my loved ones to come to me.
There we'll all sleep, for all eternity.

So do not be afraid when God calls
You too,
For I'll leave the door ajar for you
All you do is to step inside
Into Heaven's gates when God calls you to abide

Lucille Hope

BEING THERE

The role of a mother it appears
Is to give and take through all the years.
To give with love, to take with joy
To play to teach to laugh to cry.

To shield, to heal, to scold forgive.
To nurture, foster, to let live
The full potential of your child.
To point the way, be firm be mild.

To speak your mind and let her know
You risk dislike - for you love her so
That when you say what's to be said
You speak with heart as well as head.

To listen, to respect her views
On life - she can't live in your shoes.
To do your best then set her free
To let her know you will always be

There for her.

Ann F Rudy

POLES APART

Flotsam of the World War they had won
washed up on foreign shores
sans friends
No country owned them:
stateless citizens

Intelligent man good education
to work to become to belong
to be British - his problem
chased its own dog tail

The wispy wife died quieter than
closing a paperback
unwashed cups dusty room
the silence pounding close
the gloom
But no-one saw

He died alone
No country owed him friendship
no return. Nevertheless
the guilt still seeks a home.

Pat Mear

BE YE BEN HUR

How right this man be . . .
I mean Mr Bob Pettit,
We know kids ride bikes on the pavements . . .
But you adults . . . that is a different statement.

Teenagers you and the rest . . . you are a pest,
You know it is far from right,
And ready to start a word fight . . . being Ben Hur,
Another person you could injure . . . him or her.

Put your thoughts and sense together . . .
Make that cycle a pleasure,
Hold your head up high . . . respect the rules,
Let others walk in peace, and anguish cease.

Prove to yourself besides others . . .
You know the ropes of law,
Keep in line . . . others have before,
And it will be you who gets respect more and more.

Anita M Slattery

SPACE CHILD

Goodbye mother goodbye pa
I'll be gone and gone quite far
Called up some girl I used to know
Got told wasn't there
So I'm left with nothing
But a trip into space
A voyage through cosmic clean air
I'm off on one cos I'm a space child
Got grunge got funk got Pink Floyd vision ears
I'm gone and out there for a little while
The highest I've peaked for ten years
hello Floyd hello Pink
Turn me round the edge of the brink
Called up some heroes from tomorrow
They were has-beens already
Out there with a handshake
Out there doing time
But the capsule I'm in's rock steady
Got tired of writing my epitaph
So I got up and turned on the telly.

Rodger Moir

MY FRIEND BORIS

My friend Boris the painter man lives across the Trefechan Bridge,
He has a heart as cold as ice and he keeps it in the fridge,
I know he loves his history and so do I do too!
But when I do my homework I come home shot and blue.

You know you've got to pay your dues if you're working class,
But trying to climb the History Hill is like sliding down a pane of glass,
He's gunned me down time and again, and still I fight and try,
But you see it's like a dual with two fighter pilots in the sky.

You know he's holed my Messerschmitt in ze engine and ze wings
I can still feel ze cannon shells as around me zhey do zing,
He is a gut Spitfuer pilot, a cunning man and crafty too,
And all this work that I have done for zilch,
He's really made me blue!

But by and by and zhat's no lie, he vill get me down,
Life is too short for me to see more bad things come to town,
What is the gain to kick me down when he can never win,
I am shot up but will pick up and that is to my gain,
Because giving in I can never do and me he can never tame!

Oh Boris can't you see I'm still as busy as a bee,
Although you think I'm balmy too,
And a clown who's out of his tree,
Can we live to fight again in ze burning sun?
Who vill be ze first man to quit?
And who ze first to run?

Thomas Hartley

HOW GREAT THOU ART

Sir Andrew Lloyd Webber
Is going to sue
For £52, I can't believe it
Can you?

I suspect that the Cats
Will extend their paws
Say thanks for the 'Memory'
Whilst sharpening their claws

Joseph, and his Dream-coat
His brothers too
Will indulge Sir Andrew
'Any Dream Will Do'

The Starlight Express
Will continue en route
'There's a Light at the end
Of the Tunnel' Hoot! Hoot!

The Phantom will sing
As the candles burn
The 'Music of the Night'
Till 'The Point of No Return'

Sir Andrew, may I say
And I am a person who knows
It's not these headlines we want
But some more wonderful shows!

Christina R Maggs

THE NUN WHO HAD NONE

Walking down the long, lonely corridor,
She's deep in her own thoughts.
Thinking over the life she's had,
the sadness and boredom it's brought.
She is sworn to a life without,
speaking or making a sound.
The love of a man is forbidden,
Oh where is her life bound>
Now death is reaching out,
trying to grab her hand
She's regretting the things she's never done,
and now she never can.
All she wanted was children
a marriage happy and free,
but religion took over her,
and wouldn't let her be.
She's had to spend, all her life
worshipping a man she's never met
She gave up everything for *Him*
and now all she does is regret.
She regrets not having children,
a husband she could love
talking to her neighbours
and having friends to hug.
But now that chance is gone,
she only has her thoughts,
and wishes of a happiness
this life has never brought.

Donna Semark

THE MEAN MACHINE

We love to delude ourselves that our parliamentary systems
Largesse, jogs smoothly along like a well-oiled piston.
But if one is different - such as 'wop', 'chink' or a 'wog',
It would seem then that one is not so much a cog
As the proverbial spanner, gumming up the works.
Then the machine breaks down - shudders and jerks.
While its minions send out lots of paper, thereby occupying many clerks.
Slowly grind the wheels of bourgeois bureaucracy.
The machine clatters on while the immigrant begs for mercy.
He is expected to prove himself not only worthy, but sycophantic,
Meanwhile the poor sod tears his hair and becomes frantic.
There has to be another way - without compromising our principles.
A solution which allows our distinguished democracy to remain
invincible.
Every man has something to offer, whether he's Eskimo or Asian.
We should rejoice - and embrace those who would become part of this
Great Nation.

Linda Miller

THE DREAM

As I ride on midnight's
wings I hear the black winds
sing of golden desserts
and mighty kings as we ride
through the sands of these
mysterious lands. Then it
was gone - as swift as a
bird in song my midnight
ride gone I felt cold and scared
then I felt the morning sun
and my mind started to run

Katherine Whiston (14)

RACIAL HATRED

Stars were gently twinkling in the clear night sky,
Little wispy clouds were slowly floating by.
It should have been a calm and really peaceful night,
But as usual, restless humans, were thirsting for a fight.

How could the young man know they were waiting in the dark.
Knowing to reach home he would have to pass the park.
They had seen him in the club and noticed his dark skin.
The only reason needed to plan to punish him.

It did not take much talking,
And soon a crowd were walking.
Their white faces set like granite,
As their minds began to plan it.

He was whistling to himself as he happily walked home.
Without a single thought about what was to come.
Suddenly he was grabbed, and all he felt was pain
As he was kicked, and punched and jumped on, again and yet again.

It was not very long before his stillness made them pause.
They cheered and shouted yet again, as they thought about 'The Cause'.
They had always been the best, only their race was pure.
No coloured people could join in, they had just made sure.

No coloured man should have the right.
To take a white girl out at night.
He'd paid the price of thinking he,
Had the right to be happy and free.

Christine Ward

106

GAZZA MUST GO

Hello hello Gazza must go
The tabloids rant and rave
But if we're to have joy
We need the fat boy
Against Holland and Scotland The Brave

Come on Gazza your country needs you
We need a few goals and how
Our chances are sinking
So cut out the drinking
It's points not pints we need now

Gazza runs out of puff in the first match
He's driving us all round the bend
If you'd just scored a goal
We'd have made the Swiss roll
And you would have been everyone's friend

That fiasco with Cathay Pacific
And the man with the bright yellow hair
The paper's aren't wrong
Because we've know all along
Gazza's no bloody good in the air

Where are you now Bobby Charlton
Where are you now Nobby Stiles
Gone are the days when
Our players were real men
They'd have beaten this lot by miles

Alan Beasley

THE ROYAL 'BOOB'

Fergie went bra-less for a secret dinner date,
With hunky Thomas Muster, reportedly just a 'mate',
How can this be true? I'm sure she has a crush,
To be seen in such a flimsy top would surely make me blush,
Muster's former girlfriend must be frowning in disdain
as only hours earlier, she'd left on an outward plane!
Let's hope this handsome tennis ace can win a quid or two,
As Fergie's money management will really never do.
And when she follows, around the world, he'll have to foot the bill,
And should he chance to 'suck her toes', must check she's on the pill,
And when he plays his tennis and the umpire yells 'balls out,'
Will Fergie jump up in the crowd and then begin to shout;
'How dare you say 'balls out', I'm sure that it was in,'
'I am sure as I am standing here, looking oh so thin!'
If they ever live together, as often couples do,
Who will clean the dining room and who will clean the loo?
Will Fergie say to Thomas 'pass me the duster, Muster?'
Or will Thomas say of Fergie 'how did I ever lust her?'
And when the affair is over, I'm sure she'll look her best,
Jetting around the world again, seeking her next conquest,
And when she's parading her breasts again and on another cruise,
Who is protecting her little girls from all the front page news?

Olivia Lambeth

TO THE FUTURE

Tainted tales of grave delight
ends in senseless, mindless plight
Sorrowful faces eye the ground
no-one dare cry nor make a sound

What is life if not for living
What is love if not for giving
Where is God if not the maker
of all divine, the whole creator

Who gives them life to take away
to shoot their guns, and then to pray
so much fighting and killing
for so many are willing

Confused I am with the sadness I hear
for the children of tomorrow I have much fear
Can they pick up the pieces, pray God they can cope
and once again fill our world with happiness and hope.

Beverley Waddington

I

I want a man who cannot speak
to tell me all I know
I'd like a woman who cannot see
to show me which way to go.
I want to blow transparent gum
in cartoon wonderland
I'd like to be a glass apple
that no orange understands.
I want a blow up blue giraffe
to float down our street
I'd like an invisible photograph
of the girl who set the beat.
I want somebody else's thoughts
pickled in a jar
I'd like to go for a magic sail
in a doughnut shaped guitar.
I want to dance in a hurricane
wearing a black top hat
I'd like a love bite after dark
courtesy of a vampire bat.

David McShane

PUBLIC 'FLEECED' BY OSTRICH FARM
(The Daily Telegraph 19th June, 1996)

I'll pluck on the heart-strings of millions
with a tale which cuts to the quick,
how nest-eggs pledged to raise billions,
left investors puce, parrot-sick.

It began with Ozzie the ostrich,
a bird of redoubtable charms,
who cooked-up the goose of the rich,
in a collective of phantom farms.

Though this may stick in one's gizzard,
don't bury one's head in the sand,
the future's in giant lizard
and the dinosaur egg's worth a 'grand'.

José Morgan

MIRROR IMAGE

Every day such different feelings.
Every day I look the same.
Soaring high on reflective wings,
Inside glass heart burns cleansing flame.

My mind a surface of blue ice,
as dense as dense can be.
Every thought locked in a vice.
In every object myself I see.

To find my God,
I'm on a pilgrimage.
Why my life so slipshod,
I'm just a mirror image.

Alex Southgate (13)

ALTERED PERCEPTIONS

What is a racialist? It's very hard to say
As names and demarcation lines widen every day.
Once it was the Nazis (who of course were socialist)
Benito spoke for the common-man (which translates as Fascist)

Fathers, sons and brothers died on the fields of war,
Did any of them really know what they were dying for?
They did not die to save the Jews (we knew nothing of their plight)
Jerry was the enemy, 'twas simply die or fight.

We knew Flynn and Audie Murphy really won the war,
Now we're told these simple facts are not true anymore.
History is re-written into something large and grand,
We fought (they say) against racism and not for Old England.

Is it the same as racist? It's a puzzle through and through
For Bernie Grant our MP says (and so it must be true)
'A simple way to pick them out, as plain as day from night
It's another name for Englishman, as final proof he's white.'

Ronald Guest

THE CANDLE FLAME

A sun hung in the empty sky, a dead sea flowed below,
An empty town stood witness to a people long ago.
Once there had been a future, a way ahead for all,
But now disease had taken those who had survived the wars.
The chemicals in weed sown ground, the thick smog in the air,
The dead plants and trees around the world, pollution everywhere.
Why couldn't Man just get it right, why couldn't he just try,
To live in peace with nature, like the birds do with the sky.
But all through time he got it wrong and *never* got it right,
The end came with a whimper, a fading candle in the night.

Paul Sanders

111

WHEN I'M GONE

Here I am, me lying here
Quite alone except for the deer
They come and eat all the flowers
And talk to me about all the
happy hours.
And here come all the little rabbits
And they tell me
All about their little habits
It's peaceful here
As you can see
But I miss you both
       Tweedle Dum and Tweedle Dee

Sallie Sarjant Tugwell

DAY DREAMING

As I sit here numb in the tired classroom
My mind often slips away to a Knoydart Corrie
Which sang to me the sweetest song
And made my soul leap in my aching body.
The Corrie,
Encircled by a ridge that cut into the sky
Making it bleed cloud
That spilt down in a silent torrent
For the landscape possessed a harsh and dangerous beauty
But a beauty that moved me . . .
Like a vast picture it lay before me
One of nature's masterpieces framed in a gallery of mountains
But, here I sit with only mountains of work
And a hope that one day I will return.

Colin A Clouston

DID YOU KNOW?

I carried you when you were tired and worn
I dried your eyes as the tears were born
I brushed them away with a gentle kiss
Our love you will always feel, not miss.

I sit so close just willing you
To see love there in all you do
Then and only then can you know
Peace within as the pain lets go.

We live on earth as we do in school
Learning then using the golden rule
The freedom of mind the right for each one
To no-one does another belong.

Each has a right, a path, a way
Tho' we linger, doubt and stray
But in the end if we do our best
With a caring mind you pass the test.

At the end of the journey you pass along
Your failures most times were what made you strong
But no-one will judge the things you have done
As good and bad is the picture you spun.

Val Lacey

MR CHAMP

Drips of time fall into place,
Logic in the speedy pace,
Weakened by his yearning duel,
Mounted pressure becomes gruel,
When weighted in his sight,
Is the golden limelight.

Anna Beland

LIMERICKS

Young folks, old folks
Everybody come
To our little party
And we will have some fun
Bring along the apples
Sit down upon the floor
And you will hear some limericks
You never heard before
Paddy was a hairy man
He had a hairy chest
His chest was so hairy
He had no need to wear a vest
They took him to the barber
And as he went through the door
The barber took one look at him
And fainted on the floor
Miss Jean Knockabout
Would not wash her face
And everybody said
It was a real disgrace
One day she met a chimney sweep
Your face is just like mine
We'll be a pair of chimney sweeps
I think it would be fine.
Billy Spence
He had no sense
He bought a fiddle
For 18 pence
All the tunes he could play
Was Cut the Loaf and Eat Away.

Jack Howie

SUMMER

The sun outside shines strong,
And the blackbird, thrush, are full of song.

The hedges thin but now will grow,
The farmer now has seeds to sow.

The rabbit finds shelter from the heat of the day,
But danger lurks as they cut the hay.

The water shines clear as glass,
The ducks the geese have time to pass.

The buzzard soars up to the sky,
I suppose his prey is soon to die.

Summer's here I hope to stay,
Cool evening breeze and the heat of midday.

David Henry Bourne

THE COTTAGE

'We must remember to collect the keys'
This said as we near the farm after our journey.
The yearly ritual has begun. Please
let nothing be different. Dogs bark joyously,
Megan greets us and we step into the parlour.
Tea is served. Staffordshire dogs grin down
from their sentry duty on the dresser.
Bees are buzzing and the lane wears a gown
of summer. Pink campion in the hedge
leads the way to the cottage. High blue sky,
golden gorse smelling of coconut. Fledgling
Jackdaws in the barn and, at night, the owl's cry.
How I love this place. It's in my mind's eye
in the cold winter and when asleep I lie.

Eileen Peggs

PORTGLASGOW TOON

Portglasgow is a grand wee toon
　　　　It stands doon by the Clyde
　　　　The folks there are awfy guid
　　　　The welcome you with pride

The toon itself has built great ships
　　　　They sailed from shore to shore
　　　　To bring the name of Portglasgow
　　　　Great fame for this wee toon

The Newarkcastle doon by the sea
　　　　A monument to history
　　　　To guard this toon in days gone by
　　　　And all its greatest treasures

Now should you pass this way just once
　　　　Just stop and look around
　　　　The Boglestone, Boverie and The Glen
　　　　Are some of the familiar names in toon

For this wee toon is split in two
　　　　It is built like a split level
　　　　One part is at the top of Boglestone
　　　　The other doon by the Glen

Nevertheless the toon is great
　　　　So put your best foot forward
　　　　And make this a happy day
　　　　A day that you will remember

R Glass

THE STEP BACK

The horse pulled plough
drags across the turf
carving deep grooves
gaping for seeds
pleading somehow

One wrist wipes sweat
from a wrinkled brow
One finger points
to tip the hat
back from the wet

Nearby a baby's cry
a mother's smiling grace
fills the blossomed air
of sweltering odour
raining from the sky

Laughter and pulling plough
Combine like tragic lovers
caught between endeavour
and nature's emotions
its pains will disallow

me my waking thoughts
as I watch from the wall
All light freezes
            and silence halts
giving me a perspective
            on it all

Andy Mcpheat

117

THE RAINBOW

In the car park we waited -
Mum and I
At the big DIY store
Just outside of town.
The sudden downpour
Beat a hollow message
On the roof of my little car
As we sat, waiting.

To make a dash for cover
We thought the best approach,
As we eased from our spaces
And headed for the road.
Then Mum stopped and turned around -
'Look!' she cried,
And what a sight we were to see
Across the dismal car park.

A rainbow, beautiful and bright
Could be seen from end to end;
A myriad of colours,
And not enough words to describe
The feeling we felt inside -
The feeling that has stayed with me,
Still to this very day.

And now, when I see a rainbow,
I think of that day -
Just Mum and me, and the wonderment;
And I know that whatever happens
In the future
That day will stay with me -
For ever in my memory.

Christine McNaught

EPITAPH FOR OLD NICK

She lies at rest sans tomes or chalk
        No longer specs on nose.
No sheaf of essays scored in red
        (D plus for some of those)

She never favoured rock and roll,
        The Beatles drove her mad.
While as to TV soaps she warned
        'You'll go from worse to bad.'

Her garb seemed destined to repel,
        No rings nor pierced ears.
While lipstick or a shadowed eye
        Aroused for us her fears.

Yet she enjoyed a joke with us
        At howlers we would make.
That Sisera's name was Howbeit
        Or Alban at the steak.

To Sussex fair and Essex too
        The Saxons came by sea.
She'll tell St Peter what we said,
        'It ends in sex' said we.

So let there be no sigh nor tear,
        Nick's joined the Heavenly throng.
'Tis hoped they all tie back their hair,
        And none wear nails too long.

Margaret Nixon

MY OASIS

A beauty spot that I hold dear
Is where I have my pint of beer
It's called Clipstone Social Club
Lots more better than any old pub
Leaning up against their bar
Lifting up my large pint jar
The liquid slipping down my throat
I'm glad I won on last week's tote
It's helping me to buy my quota
Lots better than a drink of water
The taste of beer you cannot beat
Surrounded by those beers and lagers
Listening to those Clipstone sagas
My elbow going up and down
My sorrow I am trying to drown
Sid and Reg pour out the beers
Until it comes out of our ears
But it keeps us on our toes
When we're playing dominoes,
Clipstone's a good place to be in
Most of the people are my kin
Especially if you say cheers
With a pint of Mansfield beers.

David Brownley

FRIENDS WILL BE FRIENDS

Friends will be friends through a fragment
of courage and over a period of time
Sharing what qualities we have enjoying
Our lives from when we were young.
Julie I thought her older brother
was a bully, until she run towards
me screaming help! Help! I laughed
she was covered in water, he's only
playing, come in I've got a pair of
shorts and a top.

Then fun began I collected some
Spiders and let them loose when he
sat down to eat his food, growing
up was fun, as he got used to me.
The school trip I remember we went
to Aviemore for a week. Julie got lost
down the village streets many of
them what direction did she go? Like
the two other boys watching the water
flow, by them.

As we have got older, we laugh at
the past with a lot to say, now she
is a hairdresser always styling
people's hair. I work nights in a
hospital sometimes agency all
over different hospitals we meet at
weekends every third week as she
has a family to keep.

Monica R Rehill

TO A DEAR FRIEND

Because you are my friend
I know that I,
Have found a refuge from the
Storms of Life,
And like a rainbow's trail across the sky,
You colour all the drabness of my life.

The flowers you have strewn along the way,
Perfume my path wherever I may wend.
I guess there's nothing else that I can say,
Except give thanks, because you are my friend.

Because you are my friend, my heart contains
A peacefulness I never knew before.
I do not seem to mind life's blows and pain,
They do not seem to hurt me anymore.
I do not feel as lonely or as blue,
As once I did, when days seemed without end,
For now the days are filled with thoughts of you,
And I am glad, because you are my friend.

Margaret White

A FRAGMENTED LIFE

A fallen eclipse
in some distant sky
the beating of drums
hypnotically decline
the scars of living
between land, life and sea
most things precocious
most things are loose at the seams

Drifting momentarily
an everyday occurrence
staring at my mind's truths
a false reign of passion
life's bought and sold
an every day contradiction
the pendulum recedes
my every other dream

Clive Bell

THE WEATHER

What do friends chat about when meeting together,
The usual topic, our changeable weather.
We're never satisfied with what we've got,
It's either too windy, cold or hot.

When American cousins went to see London Town,
What happened? A peasouper fog came down.
The snow we'd like in the winter season,
Waits 'til spring for some unknown reason.

Old Gran predicts a spell of rain,
She knows she's right, her corns ache again.
The picnic we planned after weeks of drought,
Came an awful thunderstorm, a complete washout.

Frosts and cold nights seem to wait until we sow,
Our seeds for summer, then icy winds blow.
By the sea we relax in a summer's breeze,
Try having a bathe and you nearly freeze.

So accept the weather whatever the season,
It makes no sense, rhyme or reason.
To bewail what we never can change,
It's our schedule we have to re-arrange.

Kathleen Jones

THE DAYBREAK THAT GREETS TOMORROW

Don't wait for me on hallowed ground,
for that I rarely trod,
more likely find me by a shore
blissful, in my hand a rod,
perhaps contemplating my place in time,
a time ruled only by God,
I will not come to order, by prayer, deed or call,
but be behind you ever, at each and every fall
fleeting, you may glimpse me,
across a crowded street,
but bustling throngs of shoppers,
will slow your rushing feet,
you may wonder if it could be me,
then say you must be wrong,
yet the next tune on the radio
just happens to be our song,
make the most of life and living,
together, every day,
for the daybreak that greets tomorrow,
may take one of us away.

Pat Judson

A MYSTERIOUS GUEST

The frost has paid me a visit
What an unusual sight,
The fields of grass that were so green;
Are now all covered in white.

Where have all the flowers gone
Is this just a dream?
A view which is so sparkling;
However strange it may seem.

My world looks strange and magical,
The ears of corn look so unreal,
All furry like a vase of catkins;
Which are cold and chilling to feel.

My prize chrysanthemums have wilted,
And are covered in ice that sting,
We will soon escape from this chilling air;
And into a warm and colourful spring.

Marina Elizabeth Siddell

DREAMING

I had a dream the other night;
in my room without a light.
I was sitting on a cloud;
reading prayer books to a crowd.
But, as the weeks went rolling by,
I turned my eyes towards the sky;
and whispered this is not for me
for I'm a sinner can't you see?
Send me down to Satan land
where I can join his merry band.
I'm used to fags and lots of booze;
but all I do up here is snooze.
On second thoughts I could be wrong,
I've led a wasted life too long.
Although I love my kids and wife,
there's nothing more I've done in life.
So, perhaps I'm meant to be up here
to prove to God I am sincere.

Leslie Daniels

LOVE IS

What is this thing called love,
How do we know its call,
Does it come from Heaven above,
Like an invite to a ball?

Until you're bitten by this bug,
Your given path is plain,
After it has struck you down,
You will appear insane.

No doctor has yet found a cure,
It's usually fatal,
Before you know what life's about,
You wind up anti natal.

G W Bailey

IN MEMORY OF CARL

An 'individual' loved by many as a short sensitive guy with a heart
of gold,
A shirt lifter labelled by society the day he was born,
He was fond of flowers and sweet smells and a shopaholic always
tempted by toiletries and clothes,
A lover of drink, dope and chocolate,
And quite frankly when intoxicated he could be a real pain,
At times he had an OBD about cleaning,
And was the type who had cleaned an ashtray twice during a smoke,
A guy who constantly indulged in food and whose belt would never
stay still,
Bemused by romance and admittedly a Carpenters' fan,
One of those fools who'd never stop dancing until his sweat had
created a puddle,
Someone whose lifestyle would have shocked many a prude.

Carl Bridgman

NO PITY

A little help on life's way
Is worth more than a lot of pity
My little friend across the road
Waters my garden, mows the lawn
Helps clear the weeds, cut the hedges
Writes me notes that make me cry
A great little pal she has become
She even helps with my decorating.

People think these young ones irresponsible
Give them a chance to lend a hand
My spine's in trouble you see
So are my hands too painful at times
This little one's only a twelve year old
Emma her name is, gold she means to me.

So with this little one's help
My garden's a real treat
Full of bright flowers to brighten my day
So caring and considerate my little Emma
So old or young you may be
A little bit of help is worth more
Than a lot of pity.

Evelyn Farr

UNTITLED

United in a bond, so heavenly bound.
Telling each other in a lovingly sound.
The love we share, that comes from the heart.
Always knowing, we will never, ever part.

J Nicholls

DENIAL

No, no I'm not in love, no, not at all
I assure you, not the least little bit.

He is merely a friend, not even that
Strictly speaking. I see him once a week.

We have something in common, a hobby,
An absorbing hobby we talk about.

Just that, only that brings us together,
Beneath those words others are unspoken.

What shall I do when class comes to an end?
The unimaginable end is here.

I hear my voice brightly say 'Well, goodbye.'
He smiles his pensive smile. His handsome face.

Imprinted on my very soul. My love.
Yes, I love him, though I am not in love.

June Morland

A CLOSE FRIEND

I have a friend that's kind and true -
Will listen to me when my days
are blue - my friend quiet in his ways.
Is always ready to hear my calls - calls
for help in a troubled world - he can
see my heart and knows my thoughts -
he is a close friend that I never
want to lose - my friend is the
God of Love.

Rowland-Patrick Scannell

128

WHO HAS COMFORT?

Imagine to have no comfort
the basics you take for granted,
no roof to beat the weather
no door to lock no window to shut
no hope not now, not ever.

My floor is God's green earth
my roof, sometimes bright and blue
But, today grey, cold and wet
oh, sometimes how I envy you.

You have your home, your comforts
your roof and your floor,
yet still you have the need
to want even more.

Yet me, I have my comfort
to know in my heart I am pure.
I have no greed, anger or hate
I have no need to ask for more.

As long as I have my eyes
to see me from day to day,
my ears to listen to laughter
of the children at play.

I know that I have comfort
that no money could buy,
for the thanks I send up above
I have a heart full of love.

Anita Hanson

FRIENDS

The pain seared through me, it had started suddenly and burned my
                                          back and right side,
The cheerful ambulanceman dispensed his talking medicine to make it die.
Mother gave permission to the friendly surgeon to operate, to free from
                                          the pain;
'Cheer up' he winked, 'I'll perform soon.' He saw that I was under a
                                          terrible strain

'We are your friends here, feel at home and don't be afraid to make your
                                          needs known.'
I was so shy, unlike my neighbour who had made the place his own.
My schoolwork never suffered as my school friends brought homework
                                          for me to do,
'How're you? And how did it go? 'asked Thomas, 'Brains' and
                                          troublemaker Sue.

I got by with a little help from my friends, that's what friends are for,
I sat and wondered what I had done wrong for this malady to occur;
'Never mind, it's one of those things,' the nurses consoled,
'Your diet was wrong, not enough roughage,' the truth had to be told.

I sat up and listened in bed as popular songs on the radio were played,
I enjoyed, 'I'll get by with a little help from my friends,' just one of the
                                          records which the Beatles had made,
Cinderella Rockerfella was amusing and in my enthusiasm in singing my
                                          stitches broke and my wound bled,
I was scolded by the nurses and I became an obedient patient, no more
                                          to be said.
A few months later I saw the ambulanceman on the Michael Miles show,
'How kind you were to me and God bless you, I just would like you to know,
That the pain did disappear, how did you do it, was it your cheerful face?
And, by the way, what did you do with your prize winning suitcase?'

Neighbour Jones and his wife had wondered if I would be able to walk
                                          so soon,
They had brought a packed lunch for me to eat on the strike of noon,
I felt fine and would soon be out of hospital to vacate the bed,
The original pain was so intense, I had thought I would have been dead.

'Forget about hiring a taxi, I'll give you a lift home,' said Ward Sister, Kate;
'But, hurry, don't allow the traffic to build up, we must not be late!'
As I sit here with all my Grade A passes in subjects galore,
I thank my lucky stars for such good friends and could not have asked for
more.

Margaret Andrews

GOLD

Gold, I love you so much
You've got the touch
In my darkness you shine
Through, gold I love you.

No-one can persuade me
Or even say, your friendship
Blows them all away
Oh Gold I love you yes I do
You've always been there
Right by my side
With you I don't have to hide.

Gold you're so special in
My eyes, you never lie
I can always depend on
You, you're ever faithful
Ever true, I thank God
For a friend like you.

John Young

NEED

Somehow you need to possess him,
Hold his heart inside your hand.
Determine the future's manuscript.
Write the scenes and plan the plot.
Blow bubbled words into his oval mouth.

Somehow you need certainty
Ensure rose-tinted glasses are glued.
Tidy all kisses into chronological order.
Sew a million sequin words upon a tongue.
Wear a carat on the finger.

Somehow you need belief.
Open Hans Christian Anderson's Bible.
Take a prescription in double dose.
Together plant a pear tree in a garden,
Understand; you will later eat pear jam.

Somehow you need love,
Seek it naked in glowing afternoons.
Be baptised as Aphrodite's daughter.
Kiss all winter from your lover's lips.
Wonder why need never disappears?

J A Lawrence

THE BIRD NOT SEEN

First April that is mine and isn't his.
The young elms' new leaves trace
a pattern which is mostly space.

The land is varyingly green.
This amplitude
I on my own account had never seen.

High in a sycamore, a mistlethrush -
squawker, his word
for that fierce diving foot-long bird.

Renewal greens each tree.
Birds rush about to feed their young, ensuring
what he can't have: continuity.

Owl calls, a little owl.
Heard, loved, by me, it's always been.
Glimpsed just by him.
Now, it's unseen.

P S Joll

MYOPIA

On grassy field, I watch the polo-play.
The horses fast as players go for ball.
In one's blue blood and rich, I so do say.
Oh, how I love the players, saddle-tall!

On polo chair, I sit and dream of man.
A player, dazzling handsome, fair and true.
He, cultured, schooled, with skin so deeply tan
And veins of Brahmin, Boston blood pure blue.

On strápped arms, I see the ponies play.
At match which ends the season - all too brief.
'Last Chukker Cup' for winners so they stay.
Receive a kiss amid the autumn leaf.

The polo-play, he wins with lordly grace.
As Myopia's man, each heart will race.

Sandra A Merlini

FIRST LOVE

Sitting alone at the end of the bar, he moodily stared at the
froth on his jar,
Seeing her figure in lustful imagination, guts high and hurting in
sexual anticipation,
Watching the door with quick nervous glances, thinking, how many
times has he blown all his chances?
Perhaps she won't come, but she usually does, every Friday, like
clockwork, she arrives on the bus.

She always sits alone, at a table near the stage, he tries hard to
guess her name and her age,
He realised his glass was empty, and ordered another, trying to
think how he could approach her, without being a bother,
He glanced at his watch, time seemed to be mocking him, almost
going backwards, the innate stupid thing.

She isn't coming, the thought shocks his brain, but she must,
Please let her, an I going insane?
The door slowly opens, and his vision appears, as she entered the
room, he choked back a cheer.

Small and graceful, smiling slightly as she passed his chair, to
cross the room,
His breathing stopped, his senses reeling, felt he was drowning in
her perfume,
Gazing passed his own reflection, in the mirrors on the walls, past
the optics and the glasses, and other people perched on stalls,
He could observe his heart's desire, draping her coat over the back
of the chair, he thinks to himself, I know I'm in love, but she
doesn't know I'm here.

Be positive, were the words he whispered, (he'd read that somewhere
in a book), hands shaking he walked towards her, breathless, hardly
daring even to look,
Can I buy you a drink? His voice sounded strange, like a cross
between a rusty gate or a dog with a bad case of mange!
She quickly glanced up with her liquid brown eyes, and her
voice when she answered, sounded like an angels light sighs,
Her small upturned face, looking at him at last, said 'Yes thank you
so much, I was beginning to think that you'd never ask!'

J Hawkins

TO LOVE A FRIEND

to love a little is a very thing
that knights and ladies on a pony sing
to moons and winds of stars and worlds away
to bitter mischief end on sombre way

no love at all is just a gangster sport
of brawls and beauties in a winter port
but tears in shadows of a darkened hall
as fate and countenance together fall

to love too dear is simply whirlwind's tide
that sweeps such precious reasoning aside
but love and sorrow dip to drink and feed
the woman of a dream, a dream indeed

but loving you has fixed what love should be
described in sudden smiles and constancy
though I search the world and its periphery
i'll never match the friend you are to me

Francis Hinds

ALWAYS REMEMBER - I LOVE YOU

I will never have riches to leave you, on the day that we have to part
So I pray you all will have memories, to carry with you in your hearts
For all the years that we've all been together, you've meant the world to me
I've tried to be a good husband and father, I just pray that you all will agree?

All my pleasures in life have been simple, going for walks, on warm
                                                    summer days
With you and the children beside me, as through the countryside,
                                                    we made our way
Once, a field of buttercups spread out before us, shimmering
                                                    in the glow of the sun
And then to see our children's contented faces asleep, when the long
                                                    day was done!

There were times we all went to the pictures, or for walks on the shore
                                                    by the sea
These memories, are what I call life's treasures, that have brought
                                                    contentment to me
Over the years we've watched our son Ian, piece together a story,
                                                    page by page
We've seen Alison, win many trophies for dancing, and Alison and Mark,
                                                    on the stage!

Yes, all our children have qualities to be proud of, none of them, have
                                                    ever been fools
They've made us proud, (as their parents) - as they brought home
                                                    top marks from their schools,
Please forgive me, for when I've lost my temper, or if I've ever made
                                                    you feel sad
Because I love you so much my wife and children, and I've really tried,
                                                    to be a good dad!

I wonder, will I see our son David in heaven? All my loved ones, will I
                                                    see again?
If so, then one day you'll all join me, and everything will then be the same
If there are animals also in heaven, then I'll be happy, as you will agree
Because once again my faithful dog Prince, will be able to go
                                                    walkies with me.

136

And to my wife, one last thing I must tell you, because I don't know
                                    if I'll see you again?
That I have honestly, truly loved you my darling, I just pray we'll be
together again?
I just pray now, that I will be remembered, at least for the good things
I've tried to do
And if there's really a place we call heaven, then I will be waiting for you.

D Fishwick

THAT WAS RICKI SYLVA

He was not quite 5 feet tall
Yet one of the biggest of them all
He was respected and adored
When he sang 'Why me Lord'

Which prompts one to ask why Ricki Lord?
Maybe God likes his music on high
So now there's Sylva and Gold in his hoard
Perhaps that's the reason Lord why.

Though his worldly life is over
In our hearts he will be ever here
His music will live on and die never
His music will carry on and live forever.

In his snow white suit he was quite a hit
He not only loved the music he lived it
He was one of the best and so fine
So much so he became a legend in his time.

Shopping for dresses was always a hit
When Ricky got up and sang it
His charity was so well known
Now he's gone to his final home.

Malcolm Ross

137

MY FRIEND SHIRLEY

I walk with a stick, and cannot go fast
                         or go very far

Still I have a young friend, who has
                         a nice car

She takes me for shopping, or anything else
                         that I need

She types my poems for me, she is a
                         good friend indeed

Most of all, she gives me her time

So I write here to thank her, with
                         this simple rhyme.

M J Johnstone

FOOD FOR THOUGHT

Vitamins A B C D and E,
Tofu, nuts and camomile tea,
Fat free marg, olive oil,
Honey, jelly, it must be royal.
Organic bread, veggies too,
Garlic pills, seaweed kombu.
Life's a gamble, no regrets,
Where have I put my cigarettes?

Meg Pybus

WITH A LITTLE HELP

Whatever problems you may have
Be it to do with work, family or illness
Having someone you can confide in
Always seems to help the situation.

Since we met, my husband and myself
Have been each other's best friend
But over the last eight years
We've both found someone else who's very special.

Whenever we've been feeling down
Sam has been there to cheer us up
He's always prepared to listen
And he's never interrupting.

His solution to problems always work
It's a few licks and a cuddle
He never has to say anything
Actions speak louder than words.

As you may have guessed by now
Our special friend is of the four legged kind
He's our dog whose name is Sam
Thanks Sam for always being there.

Meinir

EPITAPH FOR POETS

R.I.P no epitaph for poets,
For '*Rest In Peace*' they cannot.
SAE much more appropriate,
At last themselves to be '*Stamped Addressed and Enveloped*'.

Magdelena Hill (Deceased)

MAN'S BEST FRIEND, THE END?

A dog, very well known, started to bark at me,
Yet I knew his bark, was worse than his bone.

It wasn't a bitch, I'm very sure
Because of a slight mechanical hitch, of which there is no natural cure.

This dog, a chihuahua, chased me into a wood
One might think ha, ha, that joke's good.

This was no joke, I'll let you know
It began to poke, at my big toe.

Until at last, I screamed and cried
I momentarily thought, oh blast, this dog I can't abide.

In great revenge, I kicked and cried
The poor chihuahua, could have died.

So with care and many a hand
His leg I did begin to mend
Until at last the dog did stand
Man and his best friend, the end.

Jeremy C W Bloomfield

'CLEAR VIEW' CAPTAIN

I have a trip-ship
It's parked on the moon
I may be leaving
In it pretty soon.

Mind control
To doing it right
Some things I see
To you, are out of sight.

140

It's like a tin can
It flies through the sky
I come and go in it
It's hard to say why.

Above the parallels
To clear view zone
I travel to and fro
And I'm not alone.

David Powley

DRINK

7 pints yesterday
will the nightmare never cease
Morrison - Moon I won't follow you
Friends galore evaporated in the picture
even my mother - 'not you too'

Poe drunk from bar - bar
40's young, yet celebrated through and through
what about idiot? (That's myself)
as the sick crashed the wall
enjoyed 91 - what about 2?

Drinking - silently sinking
blinking up now down and out.
Six foot under - only 22
roared an ex-drunkard now controlled
realisation triggered through the brain.

Choice is yours

'Friends forever
        V
        Drink & die!'

Matthew Ould

MY POEM

In my head words and phrases abound
wildly rotating like a merry-go-round.
Imploring me to jot them down
adjective, verb, adverb and noun.
Selection, rejection, casting aside
searching elusive ones which playfully hide.
I nurtured my choice, like a mother hen
cosseting and fussing over and over again.
Eventually satisfaction was in sight
Hopefully I had it 'write'!

An acceptance and my copyright
I was over the moon, as high as a kite.
Ordering books for my family
anticipating the moment they would see,
their mum was a poet, published what's more,
proud they would be to their very core.
The ultimate moment, my whole being expands
A royalty statement I hold in my hand.
Back in the dark ages when in my teens
I had an ambition a personal dream.
To publish some work from my very own pen
that hope was cherished for two score years and ten
Now with an editor, publisher, copyright and royalties too
my wildest dreams have been realised, hence my new scenario.

Sheelagh Evans

GOD BLESS THE BRIDE AND GROOM
(To Alexandra and Darren)

Wedding bells,
people gather
The bridegroom's mother is all
of a lather
Has anyone seen
her other shoe?
She can't find it
whatever will she do!
'Hurry up mother or
we'll be late
everyone will be waiting at
the Lych Gate'
'I've found it' 'Good,
come on do
before you take *another* trip
to the loo!'
'*No* Samantha you
can't fetch Teddy
there's no time now
we're late already'
'Look *now* what you've done
you've made *her* cry
Are you ready Gary?
Do straighten up your tie.'
Look! The cars are
waiting outside
I can see them
they've just arrived.
My goodness me, doesn't
the time fly!
God Bless the Bride and Groom
say I.

Gloria Wilkes

SET THE RECORD STRAIGHT (THE BEAT GOES ON)

Today's music is not my cup o' tea, so what would my alternative be
Elvis is my favourite I can play him from dawn till dark
Also Dusty Springfield with a voice like a 'strangled' lark
'Only The Lonely' Roy Orbison would sing
Michael Jackson, 'Never', Mick Jagger did his own thing
Little Miss Dynamite they called Brenda Lee
Only '24 Hours from Tulsa' was Gene Pitney
Dave Clark was 'Glad All Over', The Searchers had 'Needles And Pins'
Sandie Shaw won Eurovision with her 'Puppet On A String'
Rick Nelson he loved Mary Lou, The Beach Boys, Barbara Anne
Duane Eddy and guitar played 'The Guitar Man'
The Shadows played some wonderful tunes 'Apache' and 'Wonderful Land'.
The 'Green Green Grass Of Home' rendered by Tom Jones
'Can't Get No Satisfaction' said The Rolling Stone
'Save The Last Dance For Me' a real classic song
We knew all the words and always sang along
'The Young Ones' and 'Livin' Doll' Cliff sang to his fans
Marty Wilde and Billy Fury sang songs to which we danced
Buddy Holly raved on about how he loved 'Peggy Sue'
Eddie Cochrane not so happy with the 'Summertime Blues'
'Can't Buy Me Love' by The Beatles and also 'Love Me Do'
Gerry and The Pacemakers never walked alone
Then the animals entered 'The House Of The Rising Sun'
We had our transistors and dansette record players too
With Elvis singing now or never and also 'Blue Suede Shoes'
Songs and music remembered so well will they go on forever who can tell
All the old songs still played on the radio most from over 30 years ago
I really love them all they give me a sort of glow
And bring back memories of so long ago.

Sandra Witt

INDECISIVE MOMENTS

I've spent half of my life, just sat and dreaming away
And wondering just what, I could do today.

Should I start 'that job', that seem to take so very long
Or should I leave it till later, in case I do it all wrong.

I could cut the grass! Or should I paint the door
Mend that fence or perhaps just wash the floor.

There's so many things, that I could do today
But I cannot decide for the moment, what will pay.

Maybe I should, really make a start! Oh but what the hell
I'll have another cup of tea, while I sit and think a spell.

After deep thought, it maybe as well if I don't start till
                                                    tomorrow
As it's said, that jobs 'done in haste', sometimes brings
                                                    you sorrow.

Victor Travis

BE HAPPY

Nothing lasts forever, of that we can be sure,
Be satisfied with what you have and do not ask for more.
Each day is a bonus; live it to the full,
Do a kind deed every day and life will not be dull.
Be kind to one another; try not to criticise,
Time is short, no second chance, as you will realise.
Life is what you make it, put in what you can,
It will pay back double if you love your fellow man.
Every day is precious, lots of things to do,
Do not think of just yourself; think of others too.

Yvonne Powell

IN DARKNESS REIGN . . .

Was I a fool in virtue to believe
to know and close my eyes in fear
of dark that rules our hearts
for good or ill . . . it will prevail
Was I the fool
caught between lust's darker tide
tossed overturned spat from your burning eyes
heart-wrecked upon the shore of treachery
a sorrier fool . . .
to never scream at you - your jokes your smiles
your easy life founded on deceit
you read my heart an open book while secrets
unrevealed stayed in your perceptions and desires . . .
and so the fool
to smile away the pain
to never fight nor force the choice
where out of time within beyond
the darker heart imprints reborn
a saga of mistakes . . . in evil done we do again
in time again in darkness reign.

J Charles

FOX TAILS

Walking home an evening mile
I took a short cut over a stile
And crossed a field of new mown hay
The farmer had worked hard that day

Another stile, another field
Where the corn waved, ripe to yield
I paused to admire the rural scene
With splashes of poppies patterned between

Something stealthily glided the dimming light
A mother fox, weaving to keep out of sight
Her sharp eyes alert, and her sharp nose and ears
Orange coat and face laced with silver spears

She wasn't alone, for close on her tail
Four foxy cubs were learning the trail
'Free . . . Range chickens' said the note on the gate
So, perhaps they'd all come to investigate!

Bell Ferris

MONET

Waterlilies
On canvas float
Are watched by men
But not in boats
They stand upon
A parquet shore
Detecting all
But slightest flaws
Windows shine high
To set alight
To send the colours
Into flight
The critics come
The critics go
The pictures, paints
Remain on show

D T F Clifton

147

OH HOW I WISH

Oh how I wish I could play the organ
At least better than I do
But each time I find the lost chord
I find a host of others too
I've got a nice new organ
That does all sorts of things
But it doesn't always come out right
Not if you put the wrong things in
Sometimes I sit down and it's super
I feel I'm playing in Carnegie Hall
Then it all goes wrong, and I lose it
And nothing comes out right at all
I listen to others on organ
And to them I raise my hat
For however much I practise
I find I can't play like that

Oh I wish I could play the organ with confidence and aplomb
But my fingers all turn into thumbs
And again it comes out wrong
I'll get it right I know I will
All my practise will pay off
The melodies will come out perfect
And no-one then will scoff
Each chord, and pedal, ring out so true
The trills, and the expression
I'll be as good as Brian Sharp
And won't need any more lessons
But half the fun is learning
Or at least that's how it seems
And I really play quite brilliantly
Well . . . I do in all my dreams

Wendy Eaton

CURLY'S CRUEL BITE

Curly was, as Curly came
Curly, he knew, what was
And Jealousy, her game
- that bane pain

Pain struck at heart
pain struck at eye
Curly was
and bitter cried

Then Curly, he vowed
on bitten lip
That pain he knew
would clip a lip and flip

But pain, thought curly
is a two way game
Curly struck at Jealousy
the pain remained

Di, dum, di, dum, de, dum, di, da
Di, dum, di, dum, di, dum, di, de
De, dum, di, dum, de, dum, di, da
Di, dum, di, dum, di, dum, yipee

And that the end
Of Curly's whirly, Jealousy.

R J Collins

LUST - IT COMES TO US ALL

How could we ever manage without it,
this frantic urge that comes upon us all,
quite suddenly, and with so little warning.
What reasons for this animal behaviour.
A shapely pair of legs, or dimpled knees,
perhaps the flashing of a slender thigh;
a heaving breast beneath a low cut gown
that well might catch a young man's roving eye.
And in old age, what sweet memories to recall,
of joyous youthful bliss - each stolen kiss,
the perfect union when two lovers met
to become as one - whoever could forget
these wild cravings towards temptation,
the many complications - anger - fuss,
that makes such idiotic fools of us.
What other deadly sin is there to indulge
that causes one's heart so much to pound.
But frankly, you must admit it's rather nice,
and it does make the world go round.
Lust - yes, for me definitely a 'must'.

D T Wicking

OH MEN OF STEEL

Oh men of steel
Pour down on me
That muck and slag
Eaten with bits of steel
In my mouth

Sweep it all away
Clear away the works
Make the men mean
And hungry

To trudge the streets
Looking for another job
Instead of making money
They have time, to do nothing

Empty, silence, no noise
Or dust, comes from
The quiet Cleveland works and
This leaves the streets deserted

Carole Lofthouse

REIKI

You're weak
Lie down
Here's a blanket to keep you warm
I'll lay my hands on parts of your head
You close your eyes
Let nice thoughts stroll through your mind
You might feel from my hands extreme heat
May even see from closed eyes
Light and colours swishing around
In my case not only colours
But pulsating gums
Under your hand
A gentle throbbing in my right kidney
Was all the evidence I needed
Something was moving the toxins within my body
Reiki eventually
Gave me back lost energy
Slowly - surely and steadily a road to recovery
Healed me
With a gentle touch!

Marie Harte

ROBERT'S PRIDE

Family had gathered in my mother's house
When I arrived there complete with new spouse
Obviously expecting what they say
To revolve around my wedding that day.
Instead I found my new brother-in-law
Had annoyed 'my side' by taking the floor;
Loudly stating his position in life,
Excellent job, and how he and his wife
Had membership of exclusive golf club.
Membership required annual subs
Of a hundred pounds each - plus playing fees.
So that he could play with the firm's Big Cheese .
Peter, a quiet executive type,
Had obviously got bored with this hype.
Calmly interrupting (with a straight face)
He lauded these efforts in the Rat Race
But then finished with the stinging retort
'*My* jobs so good I don't *have* to play sport!'

Iris Ryder

MY WONDERFUL PC

My Personal Computer's so easy to use -
it rarely has breakdowns, it won't blow a fuse
It's been fully programmed - no software is needed
it seldom 'goes down' when instructions aren't heeded

With no floppy discs, it's both mobile and stable
For all calculations, mathematically able
Memory capacity? - None else can come near
Of computer virus I need have no fear

It's fully compatible, keen to obey
User-friendly with all, pro or lay
Its vast databases are quite simply brill
and *Virtual Reality's* really a thrill!

It processes words - whoosh! - As easy as pie
A better computer you just couldn't buy!
In new occupations, no need to cross-train,
It sits on my neck-top - my clever old brain!

Sue Millward

FAIRGROUND

Brightly coloured lights everywhere,
Screaming, shouting 'Have a go if you dare!'
In the air a candyfloss smell,
On the next pitch to the carousel.
Waltzers, dodgems and the pirate ship too,
So much on the fairground for people to do.
Bring the kids, adults come along,
The price is right, you can't go wrong.
Girls dress up to have a good night,
While dad watches the strong men fight.
Mum plays bingo with gran too,
All that's left is only you.
Terminator, horses and tropical fever,
Eating away like a starved to death beaver.
Gather together time to go home,
'Just one more go' is all you moan.
Hook a duck, the last time tonight,
And maybe a go on the magic carpet flight.

Stacey Priestley

BOMBARDMENT - HARTLEPOOL

One morn of rest, they slid their way, upon a voyage of hate.
The sea was calm, the land at rest, was blissful of their fate,
The Kaiser's fleet into the bay, upon their hateful task.

'Twas then that the early risers, saw not a fishing fleet,
                    nor whales - come to bask.

But with a crash, a cacophony of sound, unleashed from open guns,
The dust, the fires, the screams, came from the Headland's Gunnels,
As houses crumbled, smashed and burned, and children screamed in pain,

The Hun had struck first blow, on a mass of sleepy people, out there,
                    from a peaceful Cleveland Bay.

Alan Noble

TOO LATE MY LOVE

Memories, memories, happily the bad ones fade, and
just the joyous ones remain
Happiness and joy may die but love that's true can
grow again
Too late we realise the wrongs we do, the hurts
we cause, the pain of all our fears
'Tis only as we age, we realise time heals, and we
regret the wasted years.
My heart still aches, my silent tears still fall,
especially when I hear your name
I'd give the world if you and I could once more be
in love again
That precious love, so young, so sweet, so true, that
slipped away forever
Still dwells within my broken heart, a tiny speck,
a precious memory I'll always treasure.

Doreen Reynolds

OUCH!

I want to look ten years younger,
Can the surgeon's knife do that?
For my figure of youth I do hunger
The days of no wrinkles or fat.
It will cost you a great deal of money
The doctor said with a smile.
I know but I have great fortune
And being fat can never be style.
I want you to suck in my waistline.
Pull back the skin on my face.
I want to look ten years younger.
For like this I am a disgrace.
Please make me pout like a goddess,
Seductive to kiss in my youth.
Give me the *truth* of the scalpel,
With your gloves and mask please begin,
Erase and smooth out the creases,
That so callously damage my skin.
I want to see a new look,
Whenever I gaze in the mirror.
Not this withered old hag,
Whose face makes me quiver in terror.
Let me be once again in my twenties,
Ten years older than that would be fine.
Let me stand in front of the mirror,
And not see a blemish or line.
Please God do not let me grow old,
Ageing's a curse not a gift.
But with care and a fair bit of money,
I can give my whole body a lift!

G Carter

155

THE MOUNTAINS OF SIERRA BLANCA

Sweeping across the clear blue skies
Stealthily peering into nature's secrets
Dusty roads winding across the undulating range
The snow white houses of Monda
The hills of Granada
The jingle of the bare saddle on the donkey's back
What a delight to be wrapped into nature's very own!

The safari jeep treks round the mighty mountains,
The Roman bridge, the swirling smoke from the solitary house
Rising towards the fearsome steep of Sierra Blanca.
The light blue tint of the winding stream
The mighty power of the swelling river
Held back by the manmade dam.
Lush with rolling carpets of bright red poppies.

Not the sweltering heat of June
Not the hot dunes of the sandy beach,
But save me from the following jeep
Full of screeching, screaming, merry Frenchmen.
Braking, skidding, falling in a heap.
On and off the road.
The pulse is high
The sky seems nigh
A sudden stop!
Cool our nerves?
The Sangria and the quail
All seemed pale and flail
The glory of Sierra Blanca.

R Kumar

MORE PRECIOUS THAN GOLD

I miss you when you've gone away.
I'm like a sinking ship,
and yet I'm praying all the time
you'll have a happy trip.

I long for you to telephone,
then worry when you do
because I only want to say
the nicest things to you.

The times of understanding bring
a perfect happiness,
yet if we quarrel I'm so sad
and feel in deep distress.

I'm lonely when you're not near me.
Contented when you are.
I see your friendship in the sun
and every shining star.

We know each other very well
and knowing, we still care.
Love takes the best, ignores the worst
and triumphs everywhere.

The lovely friendship that we have
cannot be preached or taught.
It is more precious than pure gold
yet it cannot be bought.

I treat it with such tender care.
If nothing else, I've learned
that anything that's worth so much
must constantly be earned!

John Christopher Cole

MY THOUGHTS FOR DAVID

I have awakened early this morning,
For today, I become a bride,
In a few short hours my darling,
I shall be standing by your side.
Then, I remember, what brought us together,
Heartbreak, sorrow and pain,
You had lost the one you loved,
My friend, I'd not see again.
But time has a way of healing,
Out of sadness, tenderness grew,
The future no longer seemed lonely,
For love had blossomed anew.
And so, on this, our wedding day my dear,
Let yesterday's memories shine,
Keep them safe within your heart
Then put you hand in mine,
For the pain that brought us together,
Has given us joy, and meaning in life,
And as I make my vows today dear,
I shall be proud to be your wife.

Rosemary Remy

THE JOURNEY OF LIFE

Death is not a thing to fear,
Nor - to wonder why, in truth,
We lose the things we hold most dear,
Surrendering to callow youth;

That is not to say we ache.
To depart the life we know -
Nor wonder - at the morning's break,
Why it is - and why it's so?

We are but travellers in this realm,
A journey passed from there to here;
Sometimes - we stand fast at the helm;
Sometimes - tossed from far to near;

And so, we go upon the way,
Learning just to live each day!

Frank Probett

MY MUM

It breaks my heart to write this rhyme
But now I have no-one left at home
Our dear old Mum's
life is done, and
She has gone to see everyone
Now all her things
Belong to others
We found cards sent so long ago
It really made us feel low
From large and small things
We've had to part
Even though it breaks our hearts
A silent tear often flows
As I go to and fro
She wouldn't want us to be sad
As she has gone to see our darling Dad
And I'm sure she's saying
I'm only a door away and
It will open for you all one day
So we will see each other again
Along life's way.

Doreen Day

DREAMS

Now settle down in your favourite chair,
With your eyes tightly closed, you can go anywhere,
No fences here to bar your way,
You can travel by night, or travel by day.

Where can you go? Well you can decide,
No passport is needed, you've nothing to hide,
Just think of the pleasant places you've been,
Of people and customs, you've already seen.

You can go to the future, or back to the past,
You can make your own choice, 'cos these dreams last,
What beautiful fantasies you can weave in your mind,
It's whatever you wish, or whatever you find.

From the past it's the happy times that we recall,
From winter, through summer, and through to the fall,
And it's always good weather, and always a laugh,
There's jokes with good punch lines, and plenty of chaff.

Most thoughts are of family, and friends that are dear,
And possibly, some of them, won't even be here,
But don't be despondent at what you have seen,
'Cos anything can happen, for you in a dream . . .

Eric Hope

BREWSTER

I took you home and loved you
You're the best that I could buy
You make me so very happy
Tonight it's shepherd's pie.

You're always there to protect me
Never any hassle, backchat or grief
The bestest friend I ever had
Tonight for you roast beef

160

Some people may say you're ugly
But I just look at them with hate
For tonight my little baby
You can have a fillet steak

As long as I've got you
I have found my ideal mate
I would give to you my darling
The last thing on my plate

Theresa Corder

LEGHORN RACKETY

Leghorn Rackety lies on her side
Left high and dry by receding tide.
Her proud new topsides rubbed to the grain
Starboard shroud parted under the strain.
Warnings by radio speak of a storm
Veering to westerly, with us by morn
Leghorn Rackety cannot stand more
Sadly points bowsprit towards the shore
Hoping for visit by kind-hearted sailor
To up-end her onto a rescuing trailer.
As she lies wounded and dripping with salt
Sunlight glints proudly on copper and bolt.
Was it a tremor caused by the gale
Or did she visibly shake with low wail?
When tide in flood returns to claim
Leghorn Rackety's broken frame
She will remember happier days
When children frequently got in-stays
And shrieked with delight at downwind runs
Homeward bound for tea and buns

Colin N Howard

GOD BE WITH ME

God be my strength and saviour,
When troubles may be near,
God be my guidance with your light,
And guide me through my fear.

God be within my healing hands,
To free others from their pain,
That through your understanding and your love,
They will feel well again.

God help them to feel they are not alone,
And show them that you care,
Teach them to speak to the Lord up above,
As their problems, they will share.

And through your love and guidance,
Please give them hope that they,
Will feel the power of perfect peace,
And will get stronger every day.

So Lord please be in my mind today,
And tell me the exact words, I should say,
Help me to help others, who are too blind,
That through your understanding, you will bring
                                    Peace of mind.

Barbara Holme

OUR TOURIST HAVEN

Wales was a land of babbling brooks,
Of bright green vales and shady nooks,
Where dippers bobbed, did salmon leap
And shepherd dogs did earn their keep.
Where storm floods roared with chocolate waters,
And huntsmen searched for fox not otters.
Our land was for badger, stoat and weasel,
Resplendent for artist poised at easel,
Who'd marvel at such varied views
And strive to capture the glorious hues.
There dozens of greens with reds and yellows,
Were just supervised by swifts and swallows.
Then came the dark industrial ages,
When man poured ink on glossy pages.
His quest for coal spoiled hill and vale,
With filthy deposits of dust, slag and shale.
At first there was money for pit boss and man,
The former grew rich, the latter grew wan,
But households soon suffered from deep remorses,
As menfolk were struck down by silicosis.
For lungs filled with dust could no longer take breath,
Great pain did they suffer and untimely death.
Now neat terraced cottages were blackened with grime,
Where once man had washed them so proudly with lime,
Pastel shades were soon banished from every scene,
Whilst rivers and trout streams were dead and obscene.
Then, as green hills and vales were regaining their pose,
While the twentieth century drew to its close,
The word was relayed to each part of the globe,
And all bards were donning a 'Tourist Board Robe'.

Charles Ivor Morris

DISCOVERY

I had no form of company
No witness to what I'd found
Many temples laid before me
Ubiquitous on the ground

Sodden rustling footsteps
Through the mist soaked grass
This mist floated primal through the valleys
Echoing the past

I felt no-one had trod before
This secluded piece of ground
A place no-one had yet discovered
A place only I had found

The beauty of the temples
Amazing to the eye
A monumental achievement
Of a technology long gone by

I hacked away ancient overgrowth
My torchlight lit the windowless place
I discovered gold statues and plaques therein
Handcrafted by an extinct race

There was nothing of a size I could carry
Who could fathom the reasons for this
Eventually I continued on my way
And the valley disappeared in the mist

Fred Tighe

THOSE DAYS OF YOUTH AND MISCHIEF

Two small boys walk along the lane
Wondering what mischief the day contains
Around the corner, out of sight
They give the neighbour's cat a fright

Don't go near the river, their mothers said
They were going to the park, but that will do instead
Collecting lots of fish from the harbour
Thrown by fishermen to make them scarper

They take the fish down the chip shop
Two bags of chips and that's your lot
Spin the penny in the chocolate machine
For a bar of chocolate and change it seems

Go jumping over the muddy ditches
They fell right in, up to their britches
Covered from head to toe with mud
Go home for a bath full of soap suds

Given some icing off a neighbours cake
Sell the icing and see how much they can make
Steal the heads off the neighbours flowers
To make snap dragons which are sold within the hour

They go round the back of the local shop
Collecting the empty bottles of pop
In the shop again to collect the money
They laugh and giggle as it seems quite funny

A garden full of apples, waiting to be picked
Eating enough to make them sick
They've both been seen and start to run
To arrive back home before the setting sun

Fay Stanton

165

TIMES I HAVE WANDERED

Many the times I have wandered,
Through fields and o'er hills of green,
Surrounded by cascades of flowers,
In multiple colours and sheen,
Birds flying high in the heavens,
Others give song from the trees,
Insects abound in abundance,
The unceasing buzz of the bees,
Cows chewing cud in the sunshine,
Lambs leaping hither and to,
These are the riches of springtime,
Joys that are known to so few,
The sound of the brook as it gurgles,
And splashes its way to the sea,
Has a tinkling sound to its laughter,
As though it were glad to be free,
This picture of peace and contentment,
Brings joy to those who behold,
The beauty of these scenes of nature,
And of pleasures that soon will unfold.

Andrew Quinn

SUMMER BREEZE

The gentle summer breeze
Sometimes cool, sometimes hot.
Sometimes gentle, sometimes not.

Holyhocks and stocks
Swaying around like frilly lace frocks
In the gentle summer breeze

Sending roses into turmoil
Filling the air with scented aromas
The gentle summer breeze

166

Blowing up poppy petals like children's kites
Sweeping away cherry blossoms
The gentle summer breeze

Springing up like a diving board, then
Gently dying away in the fading sunlight
The gentle summer breeze.

G Crumpton

REFLECTIONS AT 80!

On reaching eighty years of age,
  Yet not considering myself a sage,
I often wonder where this world will be
  In the year of grace two thousand and three!

I'm sure our food explains a lot -
  It's not just raised on 'The Old Plot'!
There's additives and vitamins and such -
  Which surely do not improve it much!

Such queer things are going on -
  I really ask, 'What have we done?'
Criminals get younger and more violent -
  And where is it that they get sent?

Single rooms, their own TV -
  Hotels, not prisons, they must be!
Victims now are being charged
  Because they guard their own backyards!

Morals and values held to scorn -
  Where have these attitudes been born?
Surely it is now time to call a halt
  Even if we cannot say who is at fault?

Norman Wragg

MORNING

Morning dawns with the lark ascending,
and its sweet voice, softly blending
with the others of the sky.
Morning now is gently waking
with the chorus from on high
and its glory upon us rendering
its springtime mornings sleepy sigh.

The sun of morning warming shining
upon the dewy earth
The love of the Good Lord gently showing
in the glory of the dawn
all his goodness overflowing
with the sounds of nature praising
the beauty of the morn.

Jean Parry

TURNED AROUND

Pressure
Stress
Tension
Burnout

Uncontrollable tears
Trembling hands
Brain non-functional
Fatigue all-pervasive

A friend gives direction
Rest brings renewal
Time restores.
Thank you God for healing.

Jan Clarke

168

LISTEN

Listen to your soul
It is your free spirit
It rises with the wind
and floats across the valleys and the mountains
It bows to no man
It heeds no authority
Unfettered, unchained it is yours alone
It flies with the night
It embraces the morning sun
It flirts with the stars
and runs rings around the moon
It is your font of happiness, joy and peace
Don't let it be quenched
Don't let others destroy it
Look after your soul
and you have nothing to fear.

Catherine Venables

LAB FEVER

I must go back to the lab again, to work on the polished bench,
And all I ask is a clean sink, and no foul organic stench.
But the air's thick, and the stoppers stick, and the taps are dripping,
There are lots and lots of infernal 'spots', and slide rules slipping.

I must go back to the lab again, past the crowd in the corridor,
To the window panes all covered with grains that appear to be 'ammon chlor'.
And the noticeboard with a ghastly hoard of news-cuttings posted,
And the nauseous smell like the reek of hell, and the 'preps' being roasted.

I must go down to the lab again, where the 'finals' laugh and shout,
Where the 'inters' crush till it makes me blush to see them rush about.
And 'matrics' aspire to play with fire, until it leaves me quaking,
So I think I'll race to a safe place, though my heart is aching.

F R Paulsen

SUICIDE

I can see why it is done,
Loss of love or lack of fun.
The pain of life just too great,
Clawing, choking hand of fate.
It must be easy to be gone,
Leave the battle lost or won.
Turn and bend, leave the stage,
Bow out of life's crushing cage.
Turn your back on all the fears,
End for once those burning tears.
Knot the rope and stand on stool,
Bathe with blade in crimson pool.
Pop the pills, feed on gas,
Shatter veins on shattered glass.
Yes I can see why it is done,
For loss of love or lack of fun.

Alec D Sillifant

THE DRUMMER BOY

There was a little drummer boy
Who beat the tune of war
He marched before the scarlet line
Proud at what he saw.

Before the enemy he would stand
Ready to die for his glorious land
'Come on lads, let's win this day,'
These were his last words, his life to pay.

He fell to the ground, then lay dead
The red badge of courage upon his head,
Covered in glory, poor little lad,
So very young, so very sad.

George R Green

A LETTER TO CLAIRE

Dear beloved daughter,
regarding boyfriends - let me whisper in your ear
never fear, Mother's here, wipe that tear.
It isn't a perfect world, nor ever has it been
Adam would have told you this
when the snake, made Eve scream.

It's what you make, of what is given
impetus, enables life's rhythm.
Some, march to a different drum
putting on airs -
Others won't march without, a kick up their derrieres . . .
needing to be driven.

Amidst the circle of life, there are those
who waft on plains serene -
Ying and Yang, more their scene.
Whichever way, you choose to meander
there's sauce for the goose,
and sauce for the gander.

Now in a teenage whirl, I glimpse the jewel
who once, was my baby girl -
the grit in the oyster, makes the pearl.
My letter written with love, encloses a prayer to heaven above
one day you will become a wife -
with a loving partner, in rhythm with life.

Love Mother XX

Joanne Manning

171

THE NEVER ENDING CIRCLE OF LIFE

From birth till one, I learnt to talk,
to stand on my own, and then to walk.
I had learnt, to wash, and dress by two,
say my name address, and tie my shoe.

At the age of five, went to school each day,
learnt my A B C and my teachers to obey.
At seven years old, to read and write,
and to recognise colours, and shapes by sight.

I learnt lots more, by the age of ten,
even how without blotting to use a fountain pen,
at fifteen years, I thought I'd learnt it all,
I started work, and thought I'd have a ball.

But I've learnt much more, through the years,
What I missed out in school, I sometimes shed tears.
I often wish I could go back to school once more,
I know I'd do better, of this I am sure.

My children did not bother, to learn much at school,
now they also think, they have been fools.
They too have learnt more, through sorrow and pain,
itself the circle of life going round again.

Rita Hough

A TALE OF NATURAL CURLS

I would like all of you people
to listen carefully out there.
All you people who moan and groan
because you have straight hair.

My hair is never spick and span,
it wriggles around my face, and
every morning when I get up,
I look at myself, and grimace.

172

To keep these cursed spirals
of curls out of my way,
I have to damp and blow-dry,
every single day.

Can't you see how lucky you are
with hair straight as a die?
What I wouldn't give to be
like you, and not like I.

Ann White

ABDUCTION

An empty blackness hung over me
And for miles around all I could see
Was nothing, on that cold dark night,
Nothing, not a thing in sight.

All alone, I trembled with fear
No good to shout, no-one would hear
My feeble cries
My last goodbyes,
Be optimistic I hear them say,
But that was before I was taken away.

An object filled the sky around me
And hovered for a while quite happily,
As I stared at it and wondered in awe,
I just could not believe what I saw.

It loomed above me, large as a house,
But made little more sound than a mouse
I tried to scream, it wouldn't come -
I knew then, little could be done.

Jazmin Jones

MEMORIES OF YESTER YEARS

Strolling along St Mary Street,
My mind wandered back,
I could see a woman sitting there,
On an old wooden box,
A table stood in front of her,
A pail of water by her side,
Her hair caught in a bun,
With hairpins sticking out,
A black dress, a canvas apron tucked in front.

I'll have some mussels, a poke of buckies too,
Vinegar salt and pepper, were on the menu,
I ate my mussels, then I asked do you have a pin,
She handed one, then said 'that will be sixpence.'

I dug the pin into the buckie, took the top scale off,
Then I dug it in again, to pull the worm thing out,
Aiming it to my mouth, oh what a treat,
I'll never forget my Saturday visit
To St Mary Street.

Ella Fraser

NEWTON CHARMS

So much beauty in this town,
A view that's fit for king and crown,
This is where I build my castle,
Away from untrust, traitor, rascal.

Newton Abbot, hear my cries,
Beauty for all Devon's eyes,
Please make room for one that knows,
Your impact is a love that grows.

Let your town be my advance,
Newton, with your beauty chance,
Your vibes are gentle, calmness beams,
This town's the first of Devon's creams.

Paul Deavin

THE GOLDEN YEARS

How can I not love you,
When we have been so long together,
The happy hours we spent,
Walking in the rain,
Across the moors,
Knee deep in heather,
Just to forget some passing sorrow,
Not worrying about tomorrow,
Just living for today,
How can I not love you,
When I can still feel cupids arrow sting,
And like the birds upon the wing,
The children have flown the nest,
And in the latter years we are on our own,
How can I not love you,
When we are old and grey,
As grow old we must,
And when we are dust upon the ground,
How can I not love you,
The wind will lift the dust,
And gently blow it through the trees,
You will hear me say,
How can I not love you.

R Scott

WE DO NOT KNOW

We do not know the future
We only know the past,
But if we trust the Saviour
He will keep you to the last.

We do not know the answer
To many, many things,
But we must trust the Saviour
He is the King of Kings.

We may not know the future
But of one thing I am sure,
One day He will call us
To be with Him ever more.

James H Cory

ON THE SCRAP HEAP

I soared so high,
So young and tender,
Brought down by insanity
And the booze and fags
If I had children
They'd wear bags.
What to do?
It is a problem
As life stretches out ahead.
There is more to life
Than lying in bed,
If I write
It all down, perhaps
I will quite recover myself.

Alastair McGuinness

POETRY

How do you write poetry so many ask.
I don't know the answer, but I find it no task.
It starts in the dark as I lie in my bed
And all kinds of thoughts spin in my head.
I find pen and paper and quickly write down
All of the words for a theme I have found.
These words I am writing came to me at seven,
Nothing profound - these words aren't from heaven!
They're simply the thoughts that come out in rhyme
To answer a question I am asked all the time.
I'm no special poet, there are many like me,
The ordinary folk who will write poetry.
Sometimes I will write of the faith that I love.
Then I firmly believe there is help from above.
Sometimes I will write a few verses of fun -
A poem maybe for everyone.
I have written of death but more about life,
A poem for a wedding - for the man and wife.
I wrote of the dog I had never had,
That was the poem that made everyone sad!
I have written about Christmas and Easter too,
Those glorious events that are special to you:
I have to admit I possess a great fear -
Will the mind fail and the words not be clear?
I could write about passion, the desires of the heart,
That's the love poem that one day I will start!
I think about Wordsworth and those great poets of time
Will anyone read *my* verses of rhyme?
I do not need fame in history,
My writing is simply - for you and me.

Judy Thomas

UNTITLED

We're having a party in our street,
to celebrate VE day,
Mothers are busy preparing,
While father's are merry and gay,
Children dress up in their costumes,
All hoping to take a first prize,
but some will be disappointed,
and end with a tear in their eyes.
When they have finished parading,
and rush to the tables for tea,
their eyes light up with excitement,
when they see all the jellies and cream,
overcome with all the excitement,
too tired to eat any more,
they look up to their Mums
and say - thank you -
that was a good party for sure.

Lilian McCarthy

HOLIDAY MADNESS

When the sea frost clings and the drizzle pours
And you'd rather not be out of doors
It was then I took my holiday
In a lonely country far away
Far away far on the sea afloat
Amid the islands onboard a boat
Bound for a distance the eye couldn't see
But I didn't mind the grey - I was free

Jeannette Facchini

THE OPERATION

My Father is a pharmacist,
He has a shop in town.
He drives a vintage car
And it's never broken down.
I wish the same could be said
About my poor old Dad.
His health's not what it used to be
When he was just a lad.

Father went to hospital
To have an operation.
Wishing it was over
As the train pulled out the station.
Admiring all the nurses
He overcame temptation.
As they wheeled him to the theatre
Still having reservations.

On awaking later,
Decidedly unwell.
He had a peep at what they'd done
And promptly rang the bell.
'Nurse,' he cried, 'I feel ill,'
'I'm not surprised' she said,
'We've just been told the surgeon sewed up
something else instead.'

Christopher Smithson

THE SURVIVOR

Freezing darkness and pounding waves -
That's how I remember the terrible night . . .
The following days witnessed new graves,
Appearing within the churchyard;
And the beach was strewn with the flotsam
                      and jetsam of the wreck . . .
Not a soul has survived but I alone,
God only knows how;
Bruised and battered, with an injured neck,
Someone has found me, stumbling about . . .
All I remember is the freezing darkness
And the pounding waves -
I can't recall the name of the vessel,
Nor a single name from the crew of ten . . .
Numb, numb is my mind - the silent graves
Hide their secret;
                  I even don't know my name . . .

Daniela M Davey

QUESTION AND ANSWER

You question my presence in your scheme of things,
In the game you play man-like,
Holding your cards to your chest
To hide your thoughts and feelings,
Afraid to let go in case your options close,
You lay your cards on the table
Only when sure of your hand,
So afraid the wind might catch them,
Might whisk them into a kaleidoscope before your eyes,
Afraid to glimpse the diamond pieces of a patchwork dream.

180

But you are in my thoughts
Like the joker in the bushes,
Like a black king, like shards of ice
Melting slowly downwards,
Mirrored in a window pane,
And you are encapsulated,
For it's the hand you dealt that locks us face to face.

Beryl Stockman

OUR ISLAND

Whenever I leave our island,
For a visit or trip to town,
I always look back at the town of Ryde,
As it's lovely first thing in the morn,
I have my fun and enjoy myself,
But on rushing home in the coach,
The roar and the lights
All begin to pall,
I start looking forward to home.
When Ryde looms in sight,
I can feel the relief,
It's still there, serene and at peace.
For our isle is unspoilt,
Though quite modern,
It's quaint and so picturesque
There's no place quite like it
It seems to be changeless.
Our beautiful Isle of Wight.

Ivy Barnes

NEO-GEORDIE BLUES

I woke up this morning
And Tyneside wasn't there.
They'd kicked its dust
Off Gucci shoes
And washed it from
Their well-oiled hair . . .
And closed its yards
And docked its ships
And sanitised
Its fish and chips;
And added stuff
Quite strange to me
Like Internet technology.
And people from
The friendly past
Had up and gone
Or breathed their last,
And left behind
Uncaring types
Who vandalise
And steal and fight.
And in the dawn
I stand and shiver
And gaze upon
The foggy river . . .
Remembering the better times
Now floating down the misty Tyne.
It isn't progress I lament,
But more the sacrifice it meant.

M E Ord

182

MY SILENT WORLD!

My home is not so quiet my street is even
worse! I could never be so quiet
I think silence's a deathly curse!

My class is not so quiet, silence what a laugh!
They've never heard of it before, they'd rather
scrub the bath!

Then one day it suddenly changed the town's a
                                    quieter place!
I've never heard much noise at all not even,
                                    a tiny trace,
not a boy that's playing in the street,
or kicking a ball with his tiny little feet!
The noise is gone and silence has come for evermore,
silence can be fun!

We never hear the cabin door blowing in the breeze.
Children playing outside a game or eating a piece of cheese.
A child that's crying out aloud screaming, shouting,
a passing cloud or a storm that's brewing in the air,
a sea that's crashing or blowing hair,
we never hear no noise at all.
No clock that's chiming in the hall,
the noise is gone I hope to stay
the noise is gone hip-hip-hooray!

My home is always quiet, my street is
                                    always too.
I could always be so quiet so that would
                                    go for you!

Laura Weston (10)

183

BLANDFORD RAILWAY TRACK

It's a lovely walk surrounded by
trees and bracken.
        In days gone by the trains
went through
        There's so much to see and
you hear the birds sing
        My dog walks alongside
me with the joy of freedom
        That no trains are going to tear by
There's bridges and steps
        it's really a lovely walk
So quiet and peaceful
        yet it's all so near the town.

Janet Poulsen

SPARKLES

Little children, with glittering sparkles,
Grasping them in their tiny hands,
their faces are full of excitement
as they hear the fireworks bang.

Waving the sparkles in the air,
As the other children stand and stare,
the sparkles are now fizzling out
as the children start to shout.

Bright glittering sparkles,
are what the children like
It's a night to remember
Yes! It's bonfire night.

P Jones

184

DOWN THE TUBE

How long before I can travel on the London tube
not feeling the wanting to shout out loud suddenly:

'My son threw himself off a carpark and is dead.
How about you?'

No commuter sharing carriage space has yet leapt up,
stirred, or even murmured:

'Your words have made a difference to my life.
Challenged something in me. Thank you. I am glad I overheard.'

It is enough to stagger through the physical obstacles,
fares, non-working escalators, turnstiles, many stairs,

Senses assaulted, proximity of sweats , smells, sounds, hidden fears,
angers, uniforms, unexpected tears, unexplained delays,
closures due to unacknowledged packages, lack of rolling stock,
faults in the system, suspect bombs, buskers, beggars.

Someone has leapt onto the rails.

Do I have the courage to jump?
Do I have the courage to go on?

Wandering in these below street tunnels, hollow warrens,
Wondering if anybody takes new thoughts, redefining lines,
any sort of transformation home with them?

Behind darkened glasses, my eyes perceive others bereaved,
Looking for signposts, exits, ways out, good advice.

Grief is so different for everyone. It's individual, you see,
I am only another anonymous traveller,

Changing stations, platforms, trains,

I continue my journey.

Jean Beith

DIRTY TOTTON TOWN

Dirty Totton Town
The traffic passes through,
Images in a rear car mirror,
As the New Forest calls
And Southampton says goodbye.

Dirty Totton Town
Who recalls your beauty,
Of your gardens,
Or the bustle of your market day,
With those excellent sights and sounds.

Dirty Totton Town
On carnival day the floats pass slowly,
The children are playing and laughing,
Family having fun and young people dancing,
They are not bothered if cars pass on by,
They have found what they are looking for,
That is enough.

Patrick Art Cooper-Duffy

KEN'S ROOM

How does life go on when you lose someone you love.
Someone so young taken by the greatest God above,
There's a space in our hearts and a space in our home
It's times like these when I feel completely alone.

I'll just go upstairs and sit in your room,
I get so sad and all too soon,
But then I can smell you, it's as though you are here,
The air in this room will never be clear.

Where are you now are you looking at me,
Send me a sign and set my heart free.
I'll always love you, and miss you so much,
Oh what I'd give just for your touch.

Then I look all around me, and I know you are here,
And I feel so calm now and I'm free of fear,
You'll always be with me, my darling Ken,
It's not a matter of seeing you again, it's
Just a case of when.

Ando

ABUSED CHILDREN

Oh when are we going to stop,
These children being beaten to death,
Why doesn't someone notice their plight,
Before they draw their last breath.
Such cruelty is a sin against God,
And it's disgraceful as well,
That some people know when it happens,
But are too uncaring to tell,
The terrible anguish these children endure
Because they can't help themselves at all,
And people pass by on the other side,
With their faces turned to the wall.
Oh why do they turn away from these things
When maybe one word would prevent
A child being hurt or molested,
Intervention would be heaven-sent,
So if you suspect or know of a case,
Of a child in danger or pain,
Just stop for a while and let someone know
Then maybe it won't happen again.

C Holmes

WEST DORSET CHURCHYARD

A small grey, squat church
Crouches in the shade of ancient yews.
Leaded windows like unblinking eyes
Watch over the greensward wherein lie the serfs,
The yeomen and the gentry
Under their mounds with single crosses
Or in yellow lichen vaults.
A gull wheels overhead
Luminous against scurrying storm clouds
The first dark spots of rain darken the stones
And cleanse the Italian marble sightless face
On the effigy of a long dead warrior
Who, clad in armour, helmet beside him,
And ringleted wig framing pock marked brow,
Reposes atop his tomb.
Tangled hanks of weeds fleck the grass
Cropped by Rector's geese, still feeding on
Unperturbed by the noisy rooks
Squabbling in the leafless boughs
Of their treetop township high beyond the church,
Untidy black bodies blurring the filigree
Tracery of twigs delicately etched
Against the clouds in the fading light.
Beady, boot-button eyes ever watchful
A robin drinks from the puddled path
Of flagstones, worn crooked over the centuries
By countless footfalls of the Faithful
Going into the church, searching for
Solace and comfort within its tranquillity.

Jennifer Ackerman

COME TO MY HOUSE - PLEASE

Tell me Mr Dinosaur,
If you are free today,
Could you come to my house,
Together we could play.

I've got some dolls and I've got
Some books and I've got all sorts
of games,
Tell me Mr Dinosaur, can you come today.

I've got prehistoric models to make
you feel at home,
I've got a farm and I've got a bike
and bubbles you make with foam.
Please Mr Dinosaur,
won't you come and play.

The garden's large,
The grass is green,
The view's the best,
You've ever seen.

Oh please, Mr Dinosaur, come to my
house, this way.

Home we went, a weary pair,
His clumping feet made the neighbours start,
And now he's gone but it's
fun to think of the games we
played and the biscuits and drink.

Please Mr Dinosaur
Come another day,
Please.

Marvin Jones

HOME

When you come to the end of the road
You know you're almost home.
To see your family waiting
At the place that you call home.

It's not much to look at
Two up and two down.
But you're sure of a welcome there.
The fire is burning brightly
The kettle's on the hob
The meat is in the oven
Ready for a good nosh.
We all sit down together
Waiting to begin
Then someone shouts
It's free drinks at the Rose & Crown.
The meal is forgotten we all troop out
And leave poor Mum with the nosh to eat.

I Burnell

A BRIDE AND HER MOTHER

The day a Daughter becomes a bride
She needs her Mother by her side,
But sometimes God has other plans,
Mother and Daughter cannot hold hands.

Mother is in heaven now peacefully sleeping
A Daughter's heart is lovingly weeping,
Treasured years that they once shared
Always remembering how mother cared.

190

But Mother is there in her own way
To celebrate your special day
You know how she always said
'I will be happy when you are wed'

So Daughter when you walk the isle
On your face please wear a smile
Your smile is for your Mother dear,
Who always stays so very near,
God Bless You Dear Daughter.

Carol Shaikh

MY BOYS

Boys boys two wonderful boys
I wouldn't change them for a million joys
They give me more than that each day
Just to watch them at their play.
Bleeding knees and runny noses
Heads all pulled off daddy's roses
Laughing, fighting, funny faces
Now they're playing Olympic Races.
Change of game, it's football time
Oh! My washing's on the line.
Too late now, they've split my sheet
They run fast into the street.

Soon they're back and peace is over
Now they're teasing poor old Rover
To his kennel he has fled
And my darlings soon to bed.
Now they're bathed and both been fed
Already planning for the day ahead.
You see what I mean when I speak of the joys
Of those wonderful wonderful two little boys.

Pam Fitzjohn

LANDLUBBERS

Some gulls are born never to know the sea.
Live out their lives
From egg to fragile skeleton
On sewage farms and gravel pits,
Follow the plough
The turning furrow curling like a wave
On landlocked seas.

They are not driven inland by storms at sea,
Nor leave their nests
High on some windswept cliff
To launch themselves with silver wings outspread
On salty air,
Skimming the blue-green waves in search of fish
In boundless seas.

But still they wheel and scream. That other sea
Is all they know.
Are they content? Or do they dream
Of wilder shores; of halcyon days;
Calm after storm.
While all the years they must live out their lives
On landlocked seas.

Eileen Forrest

ODE TO MARGARET

Sitting beside the fireside, one dark and windy night,
I gazed into the embers, which were glowing warm and bright,
The flames leapt up the chimney, it was such a cosy sight,
When suddenly I realised it was. Hallowe'en this night.

The clouds they flew across the sky, they covered up the moon,
The clock struck eleven forty five, and I got out my broom.
The cat was in his basket, but up he had to rise,
To accompany me this special night, on my trip across the skies.

I wrapped up warm against the cold, I fastened on my hat,
I hopped upon my broomstick, and so did Tom the cat,
We soared up, into the skies, by Jove the wind was thin,
We rattled round the chimney pots, we created such a din.

We cruised around the skies till dawn, we greeted all our friends,
And then we floated back to earth, and here my story ends.
Except to say we weren't half glad, my old tom cat and me,
The glowing embers of our fire, once again to see.

R M Moulton

WHO IS IT?

Look my friends - who do you see?
Is it 'shell' or is it me?
You'll only find *me* right deep down,
Outside here, I'm just a clown.

Look much further and you will find,
The part of me that cares, that's kind,
It takes a journey - very long,
To only look, outside, is wrong.

Don't be frightened - dive right in,
Find the me, that's deep within,
'Cos someone down there, wants to get out,
When you need me, giz a shout.

Give me a smile and I'll know you care,
To just not bother, isn't fair,
Don't give up, I'm always here,
Talk to me, I'll lend an ear.

Build that bridge and come to me,
Now, look my friends who do you see?

Lara Allen (13)

BINGO BARMY

They've opened up a Bingo Hall
Across the road, from me,
My town's gone Bingo barmy
And it's reached my family
My brother - he's got 'dirty knees'
When he used to be so clean.
My aunts are 'two fat ladies'
And my sister's 'sweet sixteen'
My Dad keeps getting 'little ducks'
Which gets him overwrought
'Cause he's the cricket captain
And just keeps scoring nought
Our grocer's now the 'top of the shop'
Our soccer team 'legs eleven'
My cousin wants 'the key of the door'
And he's only just turned seven
Our photographer's doing 'clickety click'
It's really getting me down
I dread to think what'll happen
If the lottery comes to town

Tommy Warburton

STARTING OVER

There is an opportunity
for us all to learn
from our past.
Mistakes are for making
but they don't have
to last.
Life's knowledge
is the truth that we gain,
and our understanding,
comes from sorrow and pain.

We must seek with our soul
and feel with our heart,
and be brave enough
when the chance comes
to make a fresh start.

M Robinson

THE HOLIDAY

Our annual holiday's here again
Two weeks down by the sea
The milk's been stopped, the bags are packed
It's August the fourth, nineteen fifty-three

The bus station's full, there's nowhere to sit
Char-à-bancs leaving all the while
Some going north, some going east
The road ahead beckons, mile after mile.

Excited children with buckets and spades
Build castles of sand, complete with moats
Beach balls galore, all part of the fun
There's sand in the pockets of our coats

Clear blue skies that last forever
Our two weeks seem to go on and on
But now it's time to pack our cases
In the morning we'll all be gone

The roads are shorter going back
We're home in no time at all
Mum and Dad seem tired I know
But really and truly I had a ball

Barry L J Winters

DREAM ON

It pays to dream,
Though you don't expect it to be.
For fate may take the dream,
And let it be.

It pays to dream,
Though it may be extreme.
For fate may take the dream,
And turn it into a bright scheme.

It pays to dream,
Though it may be seen as lunacy.
For fate may take the dream
And turn it into what you fancy.

It pays to dream,
Though it may be a fantasy.
For fate may flash a beam,
And make you see.

It pays to dream,
Though it may be a vision.
For fate may flash a beam,
And shed light on the vision.

It pays to dream,
Though you may be up a creek.
For fate may flash a beam,
And send you a lucky streak.

Charles Owusu

I DREAM EVERY DAY

My dream is simple,
But meaningless to others.

Rain or shine my dream is to
Travel to India.

To open up a home for people
To come and maybe stay.

Let them express themselves.

People *scream, shout, cry, smile, laugh* and try
I want to be a part of their smile today.

Making them into someone new with
My love, care, time and attention.

Understanding the fragrance
Or a rose and life today.

Excuse me for saying this Lord
But I want to travel today,
Help the ones you left in pain.

Yes, I may dream and dream on,
But this is my dream.
My dream is meaningless to others.
Kiss them and let them die.

Parveen Dharr

THE TWILIGHT TIME

If we could go into another Twilight
Time
Where the world is free from pain
And disappointment
A world where the heavens are indigo blue
All day
With peace and love around us and
Time means nothing there
It is a place where no wars can begin
No tears or sadness for the people
Who have lost loved ones
It would be a world where we could
Feel free from disappointment
We could throw all broken dreams
To the wind
And start to live again in this
Endless time of life
Where people have got time for each
Other
And to mend their broken hearts
So we can bring down the barriers
What we put around us
And let the others know that
Each and everyone of us need
The love
What this new world could bring

Dee Lean

IN DEFENCE OF THE FALLEN

On the hill above the town
Our Cenotaph still gazes down
A monument to those we knew
So many, many years ago.
As I read the names of mates
Burnt to death in flying crates
Remembering all our battles won
On village green!
In exam room!
Our future then was very bright
Before the conflict that unites.
How proud we were, when home on leave
Knocking 'em back in the 'Cheshire Cheese'
Drinking a toast to our absent friends
In desert sands, in foreign lands
Better that our armies marred
Than the face of Britain
Should ever be scarred.
But our Cenotaph is now disgraced
Mostly covered in plastic paint
The efforts of some youthful yob
Alas poor lad he never knew
The men whose names he desecrates
If he had, I'm very sure
He'd never dare to break the law!

George Kitchen

MY BURMESE BOY - BAGGY

I'll never forget last summer, 1994
You looked so ill, I found you upon the floor
I rushed you to the vet
Will he be alright, I said
He looked at you without much hope
Let's not make promises yet
So, I took you home again
I nursed you through the day
But, you only seemed to get worse
Don't let him die, I'd pray
You lost so much weight
you grew so very tired
You hadn't even will to walk
A constant bed-change required
I force-fed you through the night
'Together' my little Baggy Boy
We put up a tremendous fight
With daily visits to the vet
And lots of loving care
It's up to you now my boy
It's up to you my pet
At last you grew stronger
You had the strength to play
We never gave up hope
You'd see your 1st birthday
You are now fully recovered
I watch you play with your toys
I'll never forget how close I came
To losing, you, my Baggy Boy.

Samantha Kerr

CIRCLES

The days replaced each other
In endless circles

I often thought of you
In the late hours
Of evening
And in the early hours
Of waking
But word never came
Of where you were
And what you were doing

Seasons came and went
Mellowed, faded
Then disappeared . . .

And now I am no longer
Waiting or hoping
For a letter in the hall
Or even
Your familiar face
In the street . . .
And I never think of you
Only perhaps
When I am weary.

The days still circle
The nights
And the months circle
The years
It's only the minutes
That know the tears . . .

M T Bridge

MAN

Overpowered by thoughts as I am
Of this species by the name of man
The mind wonders just why it is
This fascination can continue for years,
To know him, one never really does,
He is all that is bad and good because
It's his fundamental nature, vanity and pride
Maybe to explain him it's hard to describe.
His love, desire, affection and passion,
Strength, spirit, charm and persuasion
When he smiles you are lost in him
He can make your life end or begin.
The rise to fame and, downfalls are his
Yet his zeal for life undiminished by this
He goes on and tries as hard as he can
He embodies it all, and, that is a man.

E P Devereux

LEPERS

Your indifference, disdain does not worry me
You pass us by every day on the street
Your friends hide dark secrets in their souls
Cast people as social lepers never to meet.

I've done no wrong, what crimes have we committed?
Hungry, homeless, ill, poor, reasons simple to find
Reassure the selfish who only look into mirrors
Of death, disease, destruction all unknowing blind.

Enjoy false bonhomie, superficial contact, beer, cheer
Invisible eyes monitor every thought, action, deed
Suffering of innocents, truth that will never die
Pain, lies, outriders bred of vile, vindictive seed.

John Farrell

THE WAGGON AND HORSES

The Waggon and Horses now where can I begin,
A family of five have just moved in,
The kids are Dominic, Ashley and Angelina too,
The whole pub is run by Maurice and Sue,
People travel to the pub from afar,
Just to play darts in the public bar,
Teenagers, adults and not forgetting the old,
Visit to taste the meals which are sold,
In the summer people flock in tens of dozens,
People of Amwell with their friends and cousins,
The pub attracts customers in many different way,
The meals, the drink, and the buzz of busy days,
And as I am about to finish this rhyme,
I say good luck with selling beer, food and wine.

Jacey

HILLS

upon these city hills doth lie
prison walls that stand so high
prisoners marching up and down
picking up papers they have found

it's a lonely place
where they must live
thinking of the wrong they did

maybe one day
I know not when
God will let them free again
and through those heavy
gates they'll walk
facing society and the talk

Cathy Hudson

FOR LIFE IS LIKE A TICKING CLOCK

Take care of your heart,
Like your favourite clock
Wind carefully, take care
And it will not stop.

Smoking, drinking, overeating.
Time again these things repeating
We use and abuse
Till our body's drained
And all worn out
With stress and strain

Throw all these nasty
Things away
Be strong, be positive,
Try not to stray
Time to slow down
Life is not a race
Learn to take it
At a steady pace
Stop, look at life
It's far too short
That's something we know
Cannot be bought

For life is like a ticking clock
Over-wind and it will stop
So be careful, be kind
You've only one heart
Time to think good health
And make a new start.

June Downie

REVENGE

Thinking of a way to get my own back
On the folk
Who in my life
Have treated me as if I am a joke
Belittled me
Swindled me
Looked on me with scorn
All that I am waiting for
Is the day I'll be reborn
My choice of the creature whose form that I'd take
Would not for me
Be a hard decision to make
A seagull I know
Is an unusual choice
A creature that does not
Have a speaking voice
But there is one thing
That he's expert at
So enemies of mine
Get out your flat cap
'Cause you're going to need them
If ever I return
They'll be so badly soiled
They'll only be fit to burn
Hope you've got my message
My wishes made evident
I will get my revenge on all
And with regards each wish will be sent

J Harazny

FEELING FINE

10am at Northwich, I book on feeling fine.
We have to work a train to Stoke, down the Sandbach line.
I will be back within my day, things are looking bright.
No problems or long overtime, I'm going out tonight.
'Where's our train' I said to Fred, he gives a funny gaze.
'We have no train, we're spare today, it don't run Saturdays'
We sit about the clock ticks by, I know we'll get a run.
I'm hoping that the job we get will be a local one.

No Winsford salt trains heading up north
Without relief till we reach Carnforth
If we go that way things could be black
We may have trouble getting back
Or off to Godley that could be tiring
With loads of banks and plenty of firing
Then in walks the foreman, 'There's a train on the line'
'You're off to Dee Marsh,' 'Well that suits me fine.'

We set off up the arches with a powerful roaring sound
Sparks are shooting skyward, then falling to the ground
The hissing sound of steam, the clanking of the steels
The creaks and groans, the plume of smoke, the slipping of the wheels
Mouldsworth, Chester Northgate, things are going right
The massive Summer's steelworks coming in to sight
We drop our trucks, make a brew, then back up on our train
The vanman waves, the whistle blows, then off we go again
We're loaded up with coils of steel for some far destination
Control has said we'll get relief at Northwich Railway Station
When we arrive there's no relief they ask us to work through
The driver said 'Well I don't mind it's really up to you'
I start to smile than shake my head, he returns a frown
'I'm sorry Fred, they've got no chance, The Beatles are in town.'

Bruce Fisher

YOUR EYE'S A MIRROR

I glanced back and saw that look in your eyes
your pain was in them as I went for the door
my heart cried your tears because of what I was
doing to you.
For the first time the love that you felt for me showed
or was it because you were being left . . . alone?

Alone inside was how you made me feel
an empty building with bits of rubbish blown in
by the wind . . .
cold . . . damp and dull.
Was I to tolerate this much longer in order to
preserve you?
No, I couldn't . . .
the pain became so bad that even the wind began to
blow in the opposite direction.

Oh but that look in your eye . . .
it was like a pleading, a longing, a hope that
I would stay to keep you company
then in an instant your pain would be gone,
but what of my pain
where would I store that whilst I tended to your
feelings?

I cry to you, 'Let me go, so that I can find a way
to sweep out the rubbish in this empty house and
replace it with the cosiness of a new home.'

That look in your eye, it gives away your broken heart,
I know, because mine is broken too.

Deneaze Tyrrell

IF GIVEN ONE WISH

I'd wish for an end to religion and
all the suffering it brings
The wars, the deaths, the mental scars
that never solve anything
We'd all have just one God, just one
power of goodness and love
One single minded entity shining up
above
A brotherhood of people that unites us in one cause
That doesn't reek of indulgence one that
doesn't want any applause
Then maybe this world of ours would
unite and roll into one
The sharing of a faith believed
by everyone
But sometimes wishes don't come true
sadly this one never will
So God help us please whoever you
are
To love instead of kill

Julie Hunt

HAPPY?

I felt happy today,
For a moment,
In a sort of way.

I felt a fleeting freedom,
Allowing a liberty,
from a sort of tedium.

I felt a sense of peace,
Yielding a sigh,
It's a sort of release.

I felt a brief serenity,
Calming a spirit,
To a sort of sanity.

I did feel happy today,
for a moment,
Then,
it went away.

Pauline Jones

JUST ONE MORE TIME

Just one more time
I hear it all day long
Just one more time
Won't you sing that song,
Just one more time
Can you just read that again
Just one more time
You're driving me insane,
I'll do it in a minute
Just let me finish this
It won't take very long so
Don't get your knickers in a twist,
Can you reach up there for me
I'll get it in a minute
Can you push me in the swing
I'll do it when I've finished,
Can you just do up my shoe
Can you take me to the loo
Life must be very difficult
When you're only two.

Sue Watts

NIGHT SHADOWS

I have to face another dark night,
And fight it off all on my own.
Dare I take on this tremendous task,
If it means me going it alone?
Have I courage enough to face what is there?
This fog is terribly dense.
No man's land is a lonely place,
Time to give up this silly pretence.

Listen! Something moves in the shadows.
Coming closer to where I am standing.
I can feel its eyes penetrating me,
With haste it is quickly moving.
Whatever it is, it's close to the ground.
Maybe it's only a grass snake.
Could be something more horrible!
How much more of this can I take?

Run, run, with all of your might,
Escape this tormented place.
Release the visions, enfold in your mind,
Relax and untwist your face.
My wild imagination got away,
It ran amok in me.
Night shadows play tricks in my mind,
Come daylight, I will be free.

Denise Threlfall

THE SIMPLE POET

This page was blank just like my simple mind
Words to write I simply couldn't find
It's what some call a mental block
When suddenly I heard the ticking of a clock
I thought maybe I only needed time
To find some words that really rhyme
But still the clock ticked on and on
My mind still blank those thoughts had gone
Tomorrow maybe I'll be freshly inspired
Today I'm simply mentally tired
But if I had a brain like Wordsworth's or even Keats'
It would be so easy to imitate their feats
But they used a feathered quill not a biro pen
Did their inspiration come from the feathers of a hen
They seemed to have time to really stand and stare
At hosts of golden daffodils planted with such care
Would they find tranquillity to exercise their skill
In this day and age with no time to stand still
Would they be so clever in this modern age
Would their biro pens skim across the page
Would they write about vandalism which today is rife
Or of an amorous priest who left God for a wife
Daffodils are lovely if you've time to stare
But I had no time to plant them my garden's really bare

Norman Neild

LONELINESS

Silence in my soul.
Life throbs,
Hums around me.
Noise,
Smiles,
Laughter,
Tears,
Silence in my soul.

Silence in my soul.
Graves lie,
Stone-enshrouded.
Bird
Song,
Blue
Sky,
Silence in my soul.

Silence in my soul.
Deep dark
Wraps around me.
Soft,
Still,
Silent,
Death
Creeps into my soul.

Ruth Calder

INSISTENT WORDS!

Words -
Those magic words
That twist and tumble
Within my head
Asking for
Release.

Intruding -
On my daily life
Asking, begging.
When sorted out
They give me
Peace.

Returning -
To my consciousness
Insisting, demanding,
Where'er I am.
They never
Cease.

Written -
Down at last.
Hopefully pleasing.
Giving enjoyment.
Now they are
At peace!

Pat Rees

ME?

Me?
I am neat.
All I am is
a plate that is round
with a yellow banana skin
turning to brown
as the air devours it,
the end of the banana
sliced neatly off with the knife
that gleams on the edge of the
plate that is round.

Me?
I am neat.
I am also
the cup
with dregs of tea
left in the bottom
to lie, sloped to one side
as the table is wonky
like me, just like me
almost all . . .
but not.

Teetering on the edge
like the gleaming knife
on the side of the plate
but I don't gleam
and I am
more
the dregs of tea
sloped to one side
in the bottom
of my
cup.

Helen Pisarska

BRIAN'S NIGHTMARE

The blasted thing's gone wrong again
a Job Club member says
who is the man that fixes it
Charlie, Brian or Lez

His name is Brian, Sandra says
what is the trouble now
It won't accept the paper
and my CV is a wow

Some jobs I have to write off for
and CV's are a must
Each time I try to use it
The blasted thing is bust

Here comes our Brian so all is well
Club members shout with joy
Brian fixes it in a flash
He's such a clever boy

I've done the job and done it well
It prints one two or three
Now the job's completed
I'd like a cup of tea.

It's printing now so very well
Going like a dream
Then thick black lines come pouring out
Call Brian back we scream

A M Pearson

THE BLESSED SINNER

Bring me back my life
Oh mother of mercy!
Free me from this naked game;
As I am in strife.

They tear my soul apart,
And mark me deep within.
I was a captive of immortality,
Have you any sympathy in your heart?

My mind is clouded with impurities,
But my heart is still a virgin.
I don't want to walk any further;
As I am full of insecurities.

I wish I could plead to them;
To leave me alone.
All I want is a sacred home,
And a man who wants me
For my own.

The world is my enemy,
Where will I go?
You can only keep me sane.
I want to drink pure water;
From a crystal glass,
So I can banish all my woes.

I will believe in you,
When all my dreams become a reality.
I hope that one day
I'll be rescued soon,
And my faith in you is true.

Jagdeesh Sokhal

EXPENSIVE DREAMS

She's dreaming expensive dreams
She buys her ticket every Monday
Chooses six winning numbers
Hopes rise high to Saturday
When with the spinning balls, they fall
She would have bought a big house
With a swimming pool
She would have bought a new car
A house in Spain to holiday
A toyboy with whom to play
Her hopes are dashed on Saturday
Will rise again on Monday
With six new winning numbers picked
Think of all the bills to pay
She's dreaming expensive dreams
She will buy a great big mansion
And a private plane
She'd give a million to charity
Cure the world, help the sick
All her millions put to good use
She knows just where to spend
Pity it didn't work out for her
She'll have to try again
Lovely clothes and pretty presents
Dining out and friends to teas
What's a nice girl go to do
A millionaire, she wants to be

Alison Haysman

217

UNTITLED

I want to run but I don't know where,
I want to hide but I don't know how, to escape this ever-present fear
                                                    and loathing.
Hate, jealousy, rage, are building up, building up.
The monster awaits me, it feels the anguish running through my blood,
the pent up anger distorts the face of the old believer.
Insomnia and ugliness rule but, appear sweet on the outside.
The days are relentless.
Running away, running away, from what I wonder?
Fear of failure, or worse, fear of the monster awakening inside of me.
Where can I run . . . nowhere
Where can I hide . . . nowhere
The monster keeps rattling his cage, he wants out!

Perhaps in time the cage will rust and set the monster free, or perhaps
                                                    the monster
will break its cage and escape its own personal hell.

Rachel Todd

ASPIRING DREAM

I dreamt about a cottage fine
A place to sleep and wine and dine
With beams of oak and open fire
Chimney smoking in a spire
A thatch above to form a roof
And lots of love, now that's the truth.

My every day is spent with glee
Walking tall or running free
The sky above and earth below
Many blessings on me bestow
Such a life cannot be found
But worth a fortune I'll be bound.

218

Rivers meander through the glens
Where wispy willows sing sweet amens
The flowers dancing in the breeze
Make marry circles round the trees
Nature is a wondrous thing
Blossoms grow and birds do sing

I'm glad to be a part of this
And sit and dream in utter bliss.

Marion Pollitt

LONELINESS AND REGRETS

Tears of indiscretion,
                        mastery of fate.
Echoes of a searching soul
For minds to contemplate.

Nowhere left to wander now,
                          along the narrowing road
For dusk, he turns and nightly conquers
my humble thoughts abode.

But, love she lingers on,
Grasping straws she cannot see
An empty feeling deep inside is all you've given me
Nothing sweet for memory, or sour that I can hate
but constantly I hear the echoes of a lonely heart
How they reverberate

Tears of indiscretion,
                        mastery of fate
Echoes of a searching soul
For minds to contemplate.

J Dell

THE CHRISTMAS LIGHT

The Christmas tree ablaze with light
Emerald-green velvet, its jewels so bright

Crowds of people gather round,
Singing sweetly, such joyous sounds.

Pretty parcels beneath the tree
Excited children at their mother's knee

Festive food, warm glow, good cheer,
The glistening lights signal Christmas is near.

Remember the first Christmas light?
It dazzled poor shepherds with its might

Yet led them through the long dark night
To a tiny bundle, swathed in white.

God's most wondrous gift to us;
A baby boy, named Jesus.

Once swaddled tightly, loved, protected
Yet on his sweet head, our sins projected.

Later despised, feared and rejected,
Born to die, yet resurrected.

God gave us His son to show His care,
To help us through evil and despair.

A gift so precious, beyond all wealth,
To save mankind from his very self.

So when you gaze on those glistening lights
Be sure to remember that first Christmas night.

T MacNaughton

A NATION'S FLAGSHIP

White and still in shimmering sunlight
Cold against a bright blue sky
Pointing upwards to the heavens
Seven people wait to fly

Trembling now like living creatures
Blackened cones begin to glow
As the rocket's fuel starts burning
Eager now to lift and go

Tongues of fire thrust down and sideways
As the shuttle leaves the ground
Slowly rising to the dawn sky
Shrouding smoke and shuddering sound

Turning now and arcing upwards
Leaving trails of smoke and flame
Friends and family proudly pointing
Laughing now to hide the strain

Up to seven miles and rising
Suddenly it is no more
Where there was a nation's flagship
Burning debris floats like straw

Such the price of mankind's struggle
To explore and conquer space
Now the seven souls with freedom
Continue soaring to God's grace

S A Wilson

THE PRISONER

Take a deep breath
Then open the door
Step slowly outside
You've done it before
Take a deep breath
Hold your head high
Walk a few steps
You're not going to die
Take a deep breath
Walk up the street
Your heart will beat faster
And then miss a beat
Take a deep breath
Walk slowly back
Try not to panic
You'll soon have the knack
Take a deep breath
Step back inside
Congratulate yourself
Because you have tried
Take a deep breath
Then close the door
Try again tomorrow
You've done it before

Patricia J Pratt

BEWILDERED SPIRIT

I sit here in my comfortable home
cup of tea, TV video at hand,
watching pictures in a far off land

News of Bosnia once more I see, this lady looking
out at me.
Once a lady full of pride, now her tears she's trying
to hide, a bewildered spirit standing there, no-one to
help, no-one to care, they're beating old people the
reporters say, and this old lady is the worse today.

Blood pours down her once proud face, which now there
seems to be no trace. There's no medical help, no place to
hide, pictures of fear and genocide.

Two hours later the reporter said this poor lady lies in
the gutter dead, she lays there curled up as if
asleep, why has life become so cheap.

I know with these pictures they are trying to shock
to make us all sit up and take stock.
But guardians of our own conscience, we all must be
and that's why I have to write about this old lady
that I see, and of the pictures that still haunt me,
of a bewildered spirit standing there, no-one to help
no-one to care, and in her death, the guilt we all
have to share.

May Strike

223

CONNAIRE

Oh beautiful boy,
My sweet Connaire.
Your life is mapped out
By those who care.

They will love you,
And mould you,
And hug you tight.
They will always be there
When you cry in the night.

They will talk and listen
And understand,
But you will always hold them
In the palm of your hand.

Everything they ever wanted,
Their dream has come true.
You know what that dream was,
Of course it was you.

Geraldine Rollins

THE SCENERY ABOVE

She treads gently on the scenery above, cannot break anyone's heart,
convinced that somewhere there is peace.
Her footsteps are as quiet as her thoughts; they have to be for no-one
understood her feelings.
She was a goddess in every sense, engrossed in her own dreams so that
then she was away from the hateful reality.
She was higher than anyone else, yet admired the others in the other world.
If only they were as high as her, as happy as she was; she was content as
a baby in its mother's arms.

As she moved, as she breathed, every moment was special, every moment was her last chance of freedom.
'Tread gently goddess of love
come here and take my hand
we shall both fall into a world that together we will change.'
As the sisters fell from the clouds of hope, they knew that as soon as they reached the ground their world had to be as peaceful as their world above.

Tracy Hoar

HAVEN'T GOT A MINUTE

Just a line to say I'm fine
hope you are well too.
I know the lines are few
I try to put more in it
but now I haven't got a minute,
wash the dishes, make the bed,
hurry up I have to fetch the bread,
don't forget hubby's pills . . .
Oh! Dear, there's the postman, more bills.
Back home doggie's waiting,
the kitchen window needs painting.
What about the washing! I must get it done,
bundle them in one by one.
My, my, the time has flown
not a minute to call my own.
I'll just have a coffee, take the dog
just down the lane for a leisurely jog,
time to get home for tea
if there is anything in the pantry.

Phyllis Bromfield

AT LAST PEACE IS FOUND

The depths of darkness follow on
The end is near I can't be wrong.
Falling into space it really feels like I'm in a race,
My past flashes before my eyes
But it's not too sad because I want to die.
Pain is all that I cannot bear,
But death doesn't give me a scare
The end is near I do not care.
Into the darkness I still fall
Then in the distance someone calls
No it can't be it's breaking all the rules.
I'm nearly there I can see the light
But I hear somebody calling
No, it can't be right, this is 'my' time I want to die tonight.
The voice comes again I can't hear the words
I'm suspended in space not knowing which way to turn.
The lights just ahead the darkness far behind
I want to go to the light it looks welcoming and kind,
And there happiness I might find.
The voice is still there calling me back,
Back into space retracing my tracks
I'm fighting this voice by blocking it out
I can beat it I know without a doubt.
I'm moving again toward the light
        Oh it's such a magnificent sight.
A golden door that's what I see, slightly ajar waiting for me.
I reach for the door and pull myself through
The sensation I feel is completely new.
The door shuts behind me, there's a turn of a key
I feel at peace. I'm finally free.

Katrina

WHAT DO YOU SEE

There he stood across the room gazing at me
I wonder what does he think what does he see
Our eyes meet fixed in a stare
Am I interested in this man do I care
I'm not sure what to do I turn away
If he speaks to me what will I say
I think I'll have another glass of wine
Just to steady these nerves of mine
As I reach for the glass I feel a hand
I turn and there he stands
He's so handsome and tall
And when he smiles it seems to say it all
But wait what does he want me for
Is he just interested in getting me out of the door
Back to his place, coffee and a cosy chat
Well I can assure you I'm not like that
His hand reaches out to touch my face
Suddenly we're alone in this place
He gently explores my face with his fingertips
Never before have I felt like this
There's something strange a feeling that's not right
I want to protect this man hold him tight.
At last he speaks 'You're so beautiful even though I can't see
Please tell me my love what you think of me.'

M Evans

DRUGS

You sit alone in a house that is bare,
Wishing that you could be happy whilst there.
So you struggle to stand and walk out through the door,
For you know in your head you can take it no more.
You go into town for you know where he'll be,
You stand at the corner hoping no-one will see.
Then when he's alone and no-one's around,
You walk up to him with your head to the ground.
You stand side by side and you think you are calm,
You ask 'Have you got it?' and hold out your arm.
You give him the money, he gives you the drug,
You slip it in your pocket making sure not to tug.
Then when you get home you sit in a place,
Which you think will be good 'cause there's lots of space.
You sit in a corner injecting heroin in your arm,
You think in your head it will do you no harm.
You think you're at home but in fact you're not there,
For when you wake up you're in intensive care.
The doctors have worked hard to give you back life,
Giving you oxygen and going through strife.
Does this teach you a lesson or do you take more,
Of the drugs that nearly put you way under the floor.

Jane Taylor

MY PROBLEM

I have a problem - now let me se,
When I grow up, what will I be?
I could join the Wrens and go to sea
But I don't really think that would be me.
In a big house, I could be a cook,
Or maybe I will even write a book.

Perhaps I could learn to be a flier
But I don't think that is my desire.
Oh! Well, I think I will just take a nap
As I sit in the sun, with the cat on my lap,
There's plenty of time my future to fix
After all I am only nearing sixty six,
I'll just be glad that the choice is free,
And go on for a while just being *me*!

J Rogers

MY HOBBY

A quiet night in with a good book to read,
Not any old book though, it's a horror I need.
From a haunted house to a creepy grave,
A terrifying tale is what I crave.
The phone starts to ring making me jump,
I've just reached a line when something goes thump.
I decide to ignore it and carry on with the book,
When at last the rings stop, I take the phone off the hook.
With nothing to distract me, I've read quite a bit,
And until I've finished, I'm not going to quit.
A knock at the door, but oh, what the heck,
I can feel the hairs rise on the back of my neck.
Time just stands still, it means nothing to me,
I thought I saw a shadow but I'm just being silly.
I've come to the end and the eve has turned light,
So I get out another to read the next night.

Sian Hartland

ROUND ABOUT

Up and down
Straight and round
Right way up
Upside down
Love and hate
Lost and found
Early late
Silence sound
In and out
Rest and play
With without
Night and day
Young and old
High and low
Have have not
Come and go
Yin and yang
Beginning end
Yours and mine
Enemy friend
Here and there
Round about
Rich and poor
Down not out!

J Morgan

OLD NICK

Lush and green the bed -
Beneath the sheltering bough
It beckons 'Old Nick'.

Army greatcoat - seen many a battle -
His only friend - hangs loose around
The frail body, to protect against the
Cruel cold of night.

His dearest Daisy was calling him
Her lovely face appearing before his tired eyes.
The final Battle was here.

Down he lay, the soft sweet earth
Yielding to his body.
No more comfort in the bottle - just the coat -
By morning a shroud covered in soft white snow.

Birds' cries pierce the silence
With shrill persistence. But no matter;
The stiff body lies cold, staring eyes not seeing.
A tear lies heavy on his cheek
White strands of beard beneath an insect crawling
From the crescent of an open mouth

Companions of the night.
A snail with silver thread inches away
And other creatures scurry from the corpse
And burrow into the warmth of the earth.

Jean Carter

WHY

People paint their windows black
for soon the enemy will attack.
Bullets and bombs whirling around
seeking their target as they reach the ground.

All around people scream and groan
as they stand amongst rubble, that was once
their home.

Why, oh why, you hear someone cry:
dear Lord he was too young to die.
Young, old, rich or poor
'He doesn't choose', this monster war.
All will suffer at his hand,
and he'll leave behind him
a baron land

Why? We ask again and again
but there'll be no answer to ease our pain.
So people of the world unite
and our windows won't be black tonight.
For *love* and *peace* can conquer all
as we build a bridge, instead of a wall.

Paula Cronick

ADVICE TO NEWLYWEDS

I always do advocate
The marriage to consummate,
In order to procreate
And also have fun;
I just cannot overstate
The great need to propagate,
And not remain celibate,
Or live like a nun.

I think they should legislate
That people should concentrate,
The whole world to populate
With babies so small;
Though scientists may simulate,
The way that we recreate,
They simply can't imitate
The joy of it all.

I know it's quite intimate
And sometimes quite intricate,
When two people demonstrate
Their undying love;
But when we all congregate,
In order to celebrate,
Let happiness permeate
The world from above.

Freddy McDonnell

XMAS IN LONDON

In London at Xmas
Remember
That's the season of
Goodwill
When strangers smile
and greet
Each other with a
warm 'Hello'
Or even the threat
Of a kiss under
The mistletoe
Pennies are suddenly
Showered
Upon the luckless
That lie in rags
In huddled heaps
Of icy doorways
Where the trickle of
Urine
Melts the ice
And the air is riddled
With God Bless You's.

Miriam Eissa

INFORMATION

We hope you have enjoyed reading this book - and that you will continue to enjoy it in the coming years.

If you like reading and writing poetry drop us a line, or give us a call, and we'll send you a free information pack.

Write to

Anchor Books Information
1-2 Wainman Road
Woodston
Peterborough
PE2 7BU